STATE, SOCIETY, AND TRANSFORMATION

Edited by Beth A. Mitchneck

WOODROW WILSON INTERNATIONAL CENTER FOR SCHOLARS

The Woodrow Wilson International Center for Scholars, established by Congress in 1968 and headquartered in Washington, D.C., is a living national memorial to President Wilson. The Center's mission is to commemorate the ideals and concerns of Woodrow Wilson by providing a link between the worlds of ideas and policy, while fostering research, study, discussion, and collaboration among a broad spectrum of individuals concerned with policy and scholarship in national and international affairs. Supported by public and private funds, the Center is a nonpartisan institution engaged in the study of national and world affairs. It establishes and maintains a neutral forum for free, open, and informed dialogue. Conclusions or opinions expressed in Center publications and programs are those of the authors and speakers and do not necessarily reflect the views of the Center staff, fellows, trustees, advisory groups, or any individuals or organizations that provide financial support to the Center.

The Center is the publisher of *The Wilson Quarterly* and home of Woodrow Wilson Center Press, *dialogue* radio and television, and the monthly newsletter "Centerpoint." For more information about the Center's activities and publications, please visit us on the web at **www.wilsoncenter.org**.

Jane Harman, Director, President, and CEO

Board of Trustees
Joseph B. Gildenhorn, Chair
Sander R. Gerber, Vice Chair

Public Members: Melody Barnes, designated appointee from within the Federal Government; Hon. James H. Billington, Librarian of Congress; Hillary R. Clinton, Secretary, U.S. Department of State; G. Wayne Clough, Secretary, Smithsonian Institution; Arne Duncan, Secretary, U.S. Department of Education; David Ferriero, Archivist of the United States; James Leach, Chairman, National Endowment for the Humanities; Kathleen Sebelius, Secretary, U.S. Department of Health and Human Services

Private Citizen Members: Timothy Broas, John Casteen, Charles Cobb, Jr., Thelma Duggin, Carlos M. Gutierrez, Susan Hutchison, Barry S. Jackson

STATE, SOCIETY, AND TRANSFORMATION

Edited by Beth A. Mitchneck

2011 Woodrow Wilson International Center for Scholars, Washington, D.C.
www.wilsoncenter.org

Cover Photograph: A corner of a building at the intersection of Freedom Alley and Soviet Street, Tver', Russia. Reproduced with permission from Rosfoto.ru, 2011; Photographed by Artur Avakov.

ISBN: 1-933549-63-7

CONTENTS

Introduction: State, Society, and Transformation   6
Beth A. Mitchneck, editor

PART I: CONCEPTUALIZING INTERACTIONS BETWEEN STATE AND SOCIETY

Chapter 1   20
Conceptualizing "Society" and "State"
Joe Painter

Chapter 2   50
Post-Soviet Power in Anthropological Perspective
Nikolay N. Kradin

Chapter 3   77
Russian Nationalism in a Post-Ideological Era
Stephen E. Hanson

PART II: INSTITUTIONAL CHANGE AND INTERACTIONS BETWEEN STATE AND SOCIETY

Chapter 4   102
Public Discourse on the Perspectives on Transition in Post-Soviet Russia: The Pluralism of Ideas in Transforming the Public Sphere
Olga Malinova

Chapter 5   126
The Transformation Decade: More State Than Society?
Gevorg Poghosyan

Conclusion 137
Beth A. Mitchneck

Acknowledgements 142

About the Contributors 144

INTRODUCTION: STATE, SOCIETY, AND TRANSFORMATION

BETH MITCHNECK

For many years, the field of Soviet studies revolved around "Kremlinology" — an area of research focused on the politics surrounding decision making in the Soviet central government and the Communist Party of the Soviet Union (CPSU). This focus resulted in a government-centered, top-down view of life in the Soviet Union. It also resulted in a view of the Soviet state that blended two separate yet highly related structures—the government and the CPSU. Research on Soviet society centered on historical and literary studies minimizing the role of general social science with the exception of Kremlinology. This was due in part to restricted access to information, including the quantitative and qualitative data sources traditionally used by social scientists. Historical and literary studies provided critically important insights into how society in general was related to and affected by state formation and the practice of state socialism and communism.

In the post-Soviet world, social scientists have research opportunities that were previously unavailable. The result of this development has been the creation of an opportunity to step back and view state and society in the post-Soviet space in an historical context. Anthropologists, sociologists, political scientists, and geographers (among others) now integrate the study of society with their consideration of the state and state processes in the region. While some recent research attributes much of current social, economic, and political behavior to the legacy of communism or to the introduction of neoliberalism, the focus of the present volume is on contextualizing state and society with respect to longer-term cultural and political processes in Russia and the broader region. In other words, a primary goal is to bring society back into the study of the state in the former Soviet Union and Russia.

The authors met during two workshops, one in Moscow hosted by the Kennan Institute and one in Durham, England, hosted by the Department of Geography of Durham University. Each workshop resulted in broad theoretical and empirical debate among the participants about the meaning of "the state" and "society" both as terms of language and as institutions. The debates suggested that states, as both entities and concepts, as we comprehend them in the post-Soviet case, are continually conceptualized, reconceptualized, and redefined. The debates also highlighted that one's positionality in terms of national identity and scholarly perspective greatly influences one's interpretation of those processes. As a result, the chapters in this book cannot present a unified approach to understanding the state, society, or interrelations between the two. Rather, the chapters reflect attempts by the authors to examine, link, and comment on a variety of perspectives, both historical and contemporary, about the relationship(s) between state and society.

The project has a number of interrelated aims. First, we intend this volume to engage an international audience of scholars in an interdisciplinary conversation about the meaning of state and society in the post-Soviet space. The state and society lens provides a look into contested concepts such as state, public, modernity, modernization, transition, ideology, political legitimacy, *perezhitki* (holdovers), and post-Soviet society itself. Second, we intend that the papers presented here move the international community toward understandings of social transformations that are distinct from the concepts of transition and democratization. Because these terms are so highly problematic in regard to translation, meaning, and experience, we found in our discussions that a focus on them diverts analysis from the primary goal of engaging the state–society nexus. Third, we aim to move scholarly attention toward an understanding of the interrelationship between state and social engagement. Previous research on the Russian state and government has led to an understanding of the indicators of the functioning of government institutions and the impact of government policy that is critical for illuminating the results of years of political and economic reform.[1] The work presented in this volume engages with these concepts but also focuses most directly on historical and social aspects of the context in which interactions between state and society occur. Finally, we aim to distinguish the concepts and terms of "government" and "state" by providing theoretical or conceptual frameworks on which to hang empirical analyses. While the process of forming this work group and working with the international group has convinced us that it is not possible and probably not desirable to have one definition of the state, all of these aims move us toward a conversation about the meaning of state and society in places experiencing significant social change.

Our work group members tackle important but relatively obscure questions related to state and society, such as: How necessary are a "strong" state and "strong" state structure to the functioning of society? What roles do the underlying social norms and structure play in shaping the state and interactions between state and society? What role do informal and daily practices play in shaping state–society interactions? These kinds of questions are underplayed in works that analyze government institutions or the state separately from society. The general literature on the post-Soviet state focuses heavily on the weak state and the implications of the weak state for democratization and marketization as well as economic performance. Some recent work analyzes linkages between government and business institutions, but attention to conceptualizing the post-Soviet state and its interactions with society within a theoretical framework suggested and supported by the post-communist and post-socialist experiences remains elusive. Our purpose is to problematize interactions between state and society in ways that embed our understandings of these interactions within broader theoretical concepts that are not imposed on the context but rather are derivative of it—meaning that they are empirically grounded and historically supported analyses.

In the remainder of this introduction, while I neither rewrite nor endeavor to distinguish the concepts of state, government, and bureaucracy, I present a view of relations between state and society that goes beyond labels of strong or weak or democratic or totalitarian by framing the analysis of the state so as to allow for variations across time and space. Concepts such as governance and network governance may augment the ways in which scholars analyze state and society in countries such as Russia. In the last part of the chapter, I review each of the remaining chapters, noting the relationships between the findings and the overall goals of the project.

LABELING THE STATE

The evolution of Russian state institutions in the post-Soviet period provides a lens into the workings of the state and the ways that a variety of actors (state and nonstate) can have an impact on social, political, and economic change. The literature on state theory and globalization occasionally finds its way into writings on the Russian state, but could also provide additional insights into concepts that have arisen to explain state behavior during contemporary globalization (e.g., glocalization and the hollowing out of the state). Social theories on the state and globalization embed the state within society and within the particular social and economic contexts where state actors function. As noted above, often the view of the state inherent in works on contemporary Russia focuses on the state as a set of government institutions and on their efficiency, effectiveness, and performance. While these indicators are all critically important for assessing the workings of state institutions and the impact of state policy on social and economic processes, such attempts to understand and improve performance will ultimately fall short of a comprehensive understanding unless a clear understanding of how those institutions work within a broader social context is also present. A broader view of the state may allow for assessment of state activity within a social context. I refer here to a definition of the state proposed by Jessop that refers to the capitalist state as a social relation and defines it as follows:

> The core of the state apparatus comprises a distinct ensemble of institutions and organizations whose socially accepted function is to define and enforce collectively binding decisions on the members of a society in the name of their common interest or general will.[2]

If one views the state as part of society and links interactions to locally contingent factors, the state can be regarded as less of an opponent and more of a partner (albeit potentially an unequal one) in the sense that state activity does not occur without some influence from society—either passive or active. Partnering still means that conflict is possible. This reorientation of perspective, toward a view of the state and its workings as mutually constituted, may result in different interpretations of state behavior and policies as well as different policy recommendations. And, as seen in the following chapters (in particular, Hanson and Malinova), the perspective that social interactions surrounding state action are mutually constituted by state and society frames research questions and analyses in ways that suggest social actors can influence the activities of state actors without exerting control that is seen not necessarily and essentially to impede market relations or reducing the efficient performance of institutions. Below, I turn to the state theory and governance literatures to argue that insights from these literatures expand our view of the post-Soviet Russian state in ways that allow for a view of the Russian state that is less bound to normative concepts from capitalist democracies.

Writing about U.S. local economic development and globalization, Clarke and Gaile observe that "local officials choose diverse paths, in part because their constitutional, economic, and human capital situations vary, but also in response to political configurations at the local level."[3] This view embeds the state within the social context of particular places and allows for the uneven development of the state and the conditions that frame state action. While globalization has been tied to the hollowing out of the state in many different contexts, I suggest that in the Russian context, concepts such as the hollowing out of the state and glocalization may explain processes in some parts of Russia and the former Soviet Union but not in others. In other words, the theoretical building blocks from one context do not necessarily transfer to another. Our workshop participants engage with this concept to a large degree (see Painter, Poghosyan, and Kradin).

Considerable literature on the Russian state during the post-Soviet period emphasizes the implications of the weak state for the reform process or state capture by business.[4] But by constructing the post-Soviet state as weak or dominated by business interests, scholars and other observers mask aspects of behavior by state agents that can illuminate the role of the state and its evolution as part of Russian society. The following brief and purposive review of the state theory literature makes the case that the Russian state at all levels is inseparable from society.

Reviewing definitions of the state as they apply to the literature on the Russian state illustrates the ideological underpinnings of much of the current literature. Labeling the Russian state as weak or captured stems from a liberal ideology and draws attention away from processes and trends that would help us better understand the state as part of Russian society (see Kradin and Malinova). We can deepen our understanding of both the activity of the state and its role in society by reorienting or expanding our view of the state away from those labels.

VIEWS OF THE STATE

State theory encompasses several heterogeneous, ideological perspectives that shape views of the state and how it functions. A liberal view conceives of the state as a supplier of public goods and a regulator of social and economic processes. The state's function is one of allocation and arbitration. Classic Marxist views envision the state as a parasitic organization or as an instrument of the ruling or capitalist class under conditions in which class conflict drives state action. Liberal and classic Marxist views of the state explain the nature of state intervention in society. When capital interests override those of social distribution or redistribution, then the state is said to be captured by capital or too weak to balance the drive for capital.

Theorists such as Jessop and Putnam shift the focus away from the state as an apparatus with discrete functions toward a broader view of the state in which it and society are interpenetrated.[5] This view of the state advances the conceptualization of the state as a social relation embedded within a particular culture and specific places. Perhaps even more important for the study of the evolution of the Russian or post-Soviet state, if one accepts that social relations vary over space and time—within and across national boundaries—then one can expect that as social relations vary over space and time, so will the state, or the expression of the state (see Hanson and Malinova).

Particular frames of the state and society, such as governance, have shifted state theory away from the liberal approach of the study of government institutions toward a more multifaceted understanding of the state and the ways that institutions and capacities of the state interact. While Jessop's view of the relational state contributed to a reorientation of state theory to consider power as enacted through the state rather than a condition of the state, the trend toward conceptualizing the state as a participant in a governance process has also produced a realignment in the way that social scientists and humanists engage with state–society relations (see Painter).

The governance literature frames the blurring of government institutions and society as one means by which state action and social action coincide to achieve sometimes-conflicting and sometimes-coinciding goals. An important thread of the literature looks specifically at the mechanisms by which the coinciding interaction occurs. Rhodes reviews the various uses of the term "governance" and not only concludes that it is not a synonym for government, but also argues for a definition of governance that embraces the role that interorganizational networks play in the allocation of resources and social control.[6] While these functions are usually considered part of government, this framing of governance places the responsibility as well as function of allocation in the realm of networks and political configurations made up of both state and society actors. Rhodes further suggests that embracing governance in this manner conceptually blurs the distinction between state and civil society because of the mutual participation in networks. Stoker also maintains that actors from outside government institutions play a role in the governance process.[7] Jessop too advocates a view of heterarchic governance that focuses on the critical role that interorganizational networks play in governance.[8] Others emphasize how network governance may not resemble democratic decision making, may result in nonmarket allocation or a lack of transparency, and creates power dependencies.[9] Perhaps state capture processes could also be described as resulting from network governance in the interests not of society in general but one or more segments of society.

In a primarily theoretical piece on network governance and democracy, Klijn and Skelcher posit that additional theorization on this topic may lead to a contextualized view of governance networks that may account for country contexts or specific decision-making contexts.[10] While much of this work is on service delivery or policy implementation, Parker's study of economic development policy frames networked governance as a mode of economic organization.[11] Parker distinguishes networked governance as resulting in "steering and coordinating," yet shows how social relations embedded within networks may coincide with networked governance.[12] She warns that, from the perspective of a political scientist, while networks may include government and nongovernment actors, they may not serve a "steering and policy-making function."[13] Her argument cautions against misinterpreting governance through networks as networked governance.

Clearly, within the literature on networked governance there is some disagreement about its meaning. The disagreement may come more from different disciplinary norms and foci than from radically different perspectives on the process on governance. For example, Jessop's view of heterarchic governance (i.e., interorganizational networked governance) focuses on how social relations and interaction create modes of governance. Parker separates social relations from the business of governance (which she views as policy making, but which others view more broadly as state–society interaction). In any case, the concepts of governance and networked governance draw attention to ways of conceptualizing the interaction of social actors (e.g., business leaders) with agents of government institutions as a process of negotiation and engagement without necessarily claiming opposition, capture, or corruption. The governance lens explains the process of interaction more than the quality of performance or efficiency of those interactions. As such, it provides a different way to analyze how state and society interact.

ORGANIZATION

The present volume is organized into two large sections: "Conceptualizing Interactions between State and Society" and "Institutional Change and Interactions between State and Society." Common to all contributions are the state–society nexus and historical and cultural approaches to that topic. While some of the contributors emphasize democracy more than others, all frame the meanings of state–society interactions around the importance of both place and time.

ENGAGEMENT WITH THE CONCEPTUALIZATION OF STATE-SOCIETY RELATIONS

The first three chapters, by Joe Painter, Nikolai Kradin, and Stephen Hanson, conceptualize interactions between state and society from a variety of perspectives. Painter begins with a review of the theoretical literature on the state and this literature's applicability to the post-Soviet context. Kradin focuses on the role of culture over time in shaping the ways that society forms state structures. Hanson's chapter on the role of nationalist ideology in shaping state–society interactions completes the first portion of the book.

Painter draws attention to the importance of defining the terms "state" and "society." Significantly, he recognizes that the Western discourse on transformation is dominated by a discourse to the effect that countries in the former Soviet Union and in Central Europe have in fact become "constitutional liberal democracies." He notes few exceptions to the conceptualization of new states in this region as having experienced a transition to both capitalism and democracy. It is also noteworthy that Painter focuses on early conceptualizations of society as a grouping of individuals living as a community either loosely or tightly connected within an organizational setting, and notes that some classical definitions of the state come close to this definition.

Painter also explains the historical derivation of notions of the state as a bureaucracy distinct from the conceptualization of the integration of state and society. He explores the role social science has played in separating analyses of state and society in the twentieth and twenty-first centuries, and develops a useful framework for thinking through the variable outcomes when state and society are viewed as either distinct or related concepts. He also suggests an entirely different way of conceptualizing state–society relations—through the concept of "stateness." He proposes stateness as a way of linking individuals and action to the realization of the state through individual actions or performance of those actions. Painter combines past perspectives on the state and on society but takes the conversation a step further to acknowledge and perhaps privilege the role that social interaction plays in defining perceptions of the state. This concept of stateness and the constant interaction between state and society through social relations may provide a critical means of (1) understanding the variable perspectives taken by the contributing authors to the present volume and (2) drawing away from the tendency toward universalism and functionalism in social science perspectives on the state in the former Soviet space and Central Europe.

Kradin draws attention to the centuries-old pattern on the territory of the former Soviet Union of living with an "oligarchic" sense of social and political organization that he considers a distinctly cultural form of state–society relations. He draws out this perspective while amplifying Painter's point that some notions of state and society include discussion of the integration of the terms rather than their distinctness from each other. By framing state formation as a historical and anthropological process, Kradin provides an example of how state formation can occur through the grouping of individuals who self-organize into state-like settings such as those discussed by Painter. Kradin frames an argument that current processes of state formation in the post-Soviet space are oligarchic in the sense that there are a variety of social processes and actors participating. He focuses on the need to think through indigenous forms of power and how they interact with and relate to forms introduced from outside—in the case of Russia, democracy. He explains cronyism and the concentration of political power within kinship or clan groups from a historical and anthropological perspective as the development of parallel systems of governance—the social governance of traditional practices coinciding or colliding with the evolution of the democratic state.

Kradin argues for historical continuity in Russia of the social governance of state practices, writing that "the phenomenon of government based on personal relations is pervasive in societies with strong clan and tribal ties. This is related to the fact that the power bearer in traditional society acts not by himself but as the representative and leader of a particular group." He points to historical continuity in the ways in which government and governance are accomplished in Russia, noting that even during the Soviet period, the linkages to clan and kin were embedded within the *nomenklatura* system. His argument includes numerous examples of the role that clan and kin play, and harkens to Michel Foucault's concept of governmentality and the importance of the technique of government.[14] In the present case, the techniques of government are inclusion and the use of personal ties based on both kin and clan relationships.

Kradin's argument relies on a conceptualization of democracy as being formed in distinctive ways by indigenous traditions of self-management rather than by some form of internationally recognized and encouraged democratic process. While some may frame Kradin's study as just another take on patron–client relations, his argument frames state–society interactions around the exercise of power through personal relationships and long-term historical clan and kin relations as a historical-cultural process. The final portion of his argument is that public opinion, and thus the Russian form of democracy, is structured through and integrally linked to clan and kin relations. Kradin's argument places both the shape of Russian democracy and the nature of interactions between state and society in a historical framework that accounts for flexible meanings of both terms and avoids the conceptual confines of necessarily considering Russian state structures as weak or strong. He contributes to the understanding of how state–society relations are both structured and mutually constituted while attempting an explanation for the particular form of Russian democracy that has developed.

Hanson's contribution focuses on contemporary political trends in Russia as a lens into the state–society nexus. He engages issues such as the embeddedness in Russian culture of certain features of Russian society such as imperialism and xenophobia. Hanson's lens is the concept of nationalism—which he deconstructs from both a historical and a political viewpoint and places in comparative perspective. He suggests that, in general, the exercise of nationalism is rooted in an interaction between intellectual and state elites in positions of power within government structures. He also theorizes that the Russian case is one in which the intellectual elites do not have a unified approach to nationalism because of the various social sources of nationalist thought. He further theorizes that the very attachment of Russian intellectual and state elites to ideologies has weakened in the post-Soviet context to the point where Russian nationalism has not developed in a coherent manner as a force in Russian political culture. Hanson provides an explanation for the seeming de-democratization of Russia as seen through the state–society nexus. The focused review of the literature on sources and impacts of nationalism highlights the modern nature of nationalism as a concept and links Hanson's work to that of Kradin, who suggests that self-organization of peoples occurred long before formal government structures existed, and also long before the realization of nationalism in any form. Hanson directly links the concepts of nation and territory, but he notes that in Russian history a general consensus between state and social actors on a single meaning of nationalism has not existed other than in times of extreme crisis.

Taken as a group, the contributions by Painter, Kradin, and Hanson engage with a number of theoretical and conceptual issues that are critical to furthering an understanding of the meaning of state and society in post-Soviet environments. These three chapters all focus attention on the relationship and interaction between social forces and state formation and between understandings of democracy as a construct of power and the particular historical and cultural circumstances within which it is situated.

INSTITUTIONAL CHANGE AND INTERACTIONS BETWEEN STATE AND SOCIETY

The final two chapters of the present volume take a case study approach in analyzing interactions between state and society within a context of institutional change. Malinova begins this section with a deep look at the case of the institutional framework for the transmission of ideas during societal transformation. She places this in the context of mechanisms of public discourse on state and society. Finally, Poghosyan uses a non-Russian case, that of Armenia, to view the outcomes of state and society interactions in the context of large-scale economic transformation.

Malinova poses a critical question about interactions between state and society in post-Soviet Russia. She takes the concept of the democratic public sphere and asks whether an abstract space has developed in which political ideas are represented and discussed. Like the other contributors to the present volume, she takes a historical approach—albeit, one looking back no more than 20 years—as a way of understanding how meaning is attributed to the production and dissemination of ideas in Russia. She notes that most literature considered under the rubric of "transitology" does not look at the production and spread of ideas. She assigns meaning to this omission—an implicit belief that the conditions for the development of a public space for political communication occur with the presence of independent news media even in the absence of material infrastructure for communication. Malinova critiques this view, suggesting that independent news media may or may not be a necessary or sufficient attribute of infrastructure, especially within an updated context of Internet communication and other digital means of communication.

Malinova conceptualizes the process of developing political communication in abstract space as one of a shift in the locus of production, interrogation, and the spread of ideas. This is an important conceptual case for illustrating interactions between state and society in the post-Soviet space. Malinova questions the very concept of normality in political communication, suggesting that the Russian context is not the context of a Western country, and thus that the entry points and the "necessary and sufficient conditions" must be regarded as potentially different and dynamic. Her ultimate query is whether in post-Soviet Russia there is evidence of a pluralist and democratic public sphere where political ideas are discussed and disseminated, and if so, where such evidence can be found. Significantly, her framing of the question includes a focus on how the presence of ideology may affect the locus and functioning of spaces for political communication. Malinova makes a wider conceptual argument about the multiplicity of social groups creating what she calls "overlapping publics" that interact in a variety of public spaces where the discussion and dissemination of ideas does occur. She sees this space as constitutive of collective identities and public opinion. She further elaborates this conceptualization by noting that over time there are shifts in the locus and nature of the social interaction occurring in these political spaces. Malinova concludes that shifts in the locus of interaction may occur even if the principal actors remain the same. She uses the example of the shifting forms of political communication during the perestroika period versus the political regimes of Boris Yeltsin and Vladimir Putin.

While most of the other contributions are interlinked around issues of history and state–society interaction, in his chapter Poghosyan considers institutional change from a different angle, engaging with the issue of civil society and the application of Western theories of development to distinctive ethno-cultural contexts. Like other contributors, Poghosyan focuses on the particular historical and cultural context that may mediate the outcome of similar democratization and marketization processes. He uses the example of labor force changes, specifically the aging of the population due to out-migration of working-age people, high unemployment, and the problem of the working poor, as his point of entry to the multiplicity of outcomes. He contributes to debates about the role and impact of democratization by pointing to real differences in public opinion about the meaning of democracy. He suggests that one important contextual difference in the former Soviet space is the actual meaning of democracy as a means for structuring interactions between state and society. He notes that Europeans think in terms of participatory democracy with actual engagement with the political process, while individuals in post-Soviet countries think about representative democracy in a form in which social interaction with the political process comes from the act of voting in elections.

SUMMARY

The work group members provide perspectives and analyses on state and society in the countries of the former Soviet Union—primarily Russia—that rely less on theories derived from Western contexts and more on culturally and historically specific analyses of important social processes. The social processes examined in the following chapters vary widely—from the development of state institutions to social engagement with these institutions, to the social interrogation of new ideas. While we provide a few answers on important issues such as the role of ideology in formation, we also encourage readers to consider a larger set of concepts with which to think through relations between state and society in the context of large-scale social and economic change.

NOTES

1 Colton and Holmes are the editors of a useful volume whose contributing authors look specifically at governance concerns and institutional developments. See *The State after Communism: Governance in the New Russia*, eds. Timothy Colton and Stephen Holmes (Lanham, MD: Rowman & Littlefield, 2006).

2 Robert Jessop, *State Theory: Putting Capitalist States in Their Place* (Cambridge: Polity Press, 1990), 341.

3 Susan Clarke and Gary Gaile, "Moving Toward Entrepreneurial Economic Development Policies: Opportunities and Barriers," *Policy Studies Journal* 17 (1989): 89.

4 See Ichiro Iwasaki and Taku Suzuki, "Transition Strategy, Corporate Exploitation, and State Capture: An Empirical Analysis of the Former Soviet States," *Communist and Post-Communist Studies* 40 (2007): 393–422; Timothy Frye, "Capture or Exchange? Business Lobbying in Russia," *Europe–Asia Studies* 54 (2002): 1017–36; Joel Hellman, G. Jones, and D. Kaufmann, "Seize the State, Seize the Day: State Capture and Influence in Transition Economies," *Journal of Comparative Economics* 31 (2003): 751–73.

5 Jessop, *State Theory*; and R. Putnam, *Making Democracy Work* (Princeton, NJ: Princeton University Press, 1993).

6 R.A.W. Rhodes, "The New Governance: Governing without Government," *Political Studies* 44 (1996): 652–67.

7 Gerry Stoker, "Governance as Theory: Five Propositions," *International Social Science Journal* 50 (1998): 17–28.

8 Robert Jessop, "The Rise of Governance and the Risks of Failure: The Case of Economic Development," *International Social Science Journal* 50 (1998): 29–45.

9 Stoker, "Governance as Theory"; Jon Coaffee and Patsy Healey, "'My Voice: My Place': Tracking Transformations in Urban Governance," *Urban Studies* 40 (2003): 1979–99.

10 Erik-Hans Klijn and Chris Skelcher, "Democracy and Governance Networks: Compatible or Not?" *Public Administration* 85 (2007): 587–608.

11 Rachel Parker, "Networked Governance or Just Networks? Local Governance of the Knowledge Economy in Limerick (Ireland) and Karlskrona (Sweden)," *Political Studies* 55 (2007): 113–32.

12 Ibid., 117.

13 Ibid., 129.

14 Michel Foucault, "Governmentality," in *The Foucault Effect: Studies in Governmentality*, eds. Graham Burchell, Colin Gordon, and Peter Miller (Chicago: University of Chicago Press, 1991).

PART ONE
CHAPTER 1
CONCEPTUALIZING "SOCIETY" AND "STATE"

JOE PAINTER

The study of state–society relations has long been a staple of political science, political sociology, political geography, and political philosophy. Yet there is no consensus on the meanings of the basic terms "state" and "society" or on how relations between them should be understood. In part this is because states and societies are dynamic and changing phenomena. Nowhere is this more true than in the post-socialist countries of the former Soviet Union and East Europe. According to the dominant Western discourse, state institutions in post-socialist countries have undergone a comprehensive transformation from authoritarian, centralized, and bureaucratic dictatorships to constitutional liberal democracies. Similarly, according to the dominant discourse, these countries' societies are changing rapidly from centrally planned, closed, and stagnant backwaters to ostensibly free and open democracies with expanding market economies and developing civic and public realms.

In accordance with the recommendations of Western governments and policy advisers, most post-socialist countries signed up for reform programs involving the rolling back of the state, the privatization of state assets, and the establishment of liberal democratic forms of governance. On the face of it, these initiatives involved a significant recasting of state–society relations, including reductions in the role of the state in economic and social life, constitutional limits on state powers, and the identification of the state and civil society as separate spheres. Interactions between state and civil society, so it was said, would henceforth occur through formal mechanisms such as competitive parliamentary elections, a free press, and an independent judiciary.

In the Soviet Union, as Vladimir Shlapentokh observes, the processes of democratization and perestroika that began in the late 1980s saw the wholesale denigration of the state by those pushing for reform:

> The advocates of liberal capitalism in the Soviet Union became committed enemies of the state. In their articles and papers they ignored the positive economic aspects of the state and other public agencies. In fact, they completely denounced the state without making a distinction between the state in a socialist society and the state in other types of societies.[1]

Shlapentokh further notes that

> when the ideologues of privatisation mentioned the state, they talked about it only as a hostile force in the economy. The state was never discussed as an important agency for establishing and enforcing the rules of the new economic system (particularly in fighting monopolies and enforcing laws); it was never seen as a promoter of science, education, technological progress or the arts. They ignored the importance of state support in certain sectors of the economy, such as transport, that were necessary to satisfy public interests.[2]

This ideological emphasis on the rolling back of the state at any price had profound consequences, including many that were unforeseen, at least by the committed privatizers. Initially, Shlapentokh argues, "the development of Russian society advanced according to the precepts of the ideologues."[3] However, the denigration of any form of state action led to a sharp decline in observance of the law, and thus, "the determination of Russian liberals to create a Lockean society while downgrading the state led ultimately to the partial restoration of authoritarianism in Russia in the 1990s."[4] One can also suggest that this process led to the re-entry of the state into economic management—albeit in new forms that once again have blurred the roles of state and society in the economy.

There are three reasons why a reconsideration of state–society relations is timely. First, the authoritarian tendencies evident in Russia under the government of Vladimir Putin and in several other post-Soviet states suggest that the "problem" of state–society relations is far from resolved. At the same time, the association between post-socialism and authoritarianism is not inevitable. Liberal democracy had been sufficiently consolidated in the Baltic republics, the Visegrad countries (Poland, Hungary, Slovakia, and the Czech Republic) and Slovenia for them to be admitted to membership in the European Union in 2004. Second, the negative consequences of the drive to privatize at any price have become apparent even to orthodox free-market economists in the West such as Milton Friedman. The neoconservative thinker Frances Fukuyama observes that Friedman noted in an interview in 2001 "that a decade earlier he would have had three words for countries making the transition from socialism: 'privatize, privatize, privatize.' 'But I was wrong,' he continued. 'It turns out that the rule of law is probably more basic.'"[5] Fukuyama's own book, *State-Building: Governance and World Order in the Twenty-First Century* (2004), is a paean to the need for state building, based on the "new conventional wisdom" that "institutions matter."[6]

The third reason for the timeliness of a new look at the subject is the relative lack of attention paid by state theorists to non-Western states generally, and to post-socialist states in particular. That the main (though still limited) exception to this pattern of neglect is in the area studies literature suggests that "general" state theory remains grounded ethnocentrically in the Western experience.

The theoretical literature in English on the role of the state in post-socialist countries is rather limited. Much of it is organized quite rigidly around conventional, mainstream political-science approaches. It is also often highly normative. This is particularly true of "transitology" studies, which typically seek to measure progress along a presumed transitional continuum from authoritarian regime to democracy, with the salutary nature of the latter taken for granted. Such studies typically lack an analysis of actual state restructuring on its own terms. Moreover, there is no single, essential "post-socialist state." While there are some commonalities, the long histories and recent development paths of state institutions have been very different in different countries, and it makes little sense to try to develop a unified model applicable to all cases. However, it should be possible to set out some general principles that might usefully inform analyses of changing state–society relations in particular contexts.

The present chapter is organized as follows. In the next section I consider how the meanings in English of the two terms "state" and "society" have evolved over time. I then focus on the idea of the state in Western political theory and examine how the state has come to be understood as a distinct organization, separate from the rest of society. I also review a number of critiques of this reification. In the next section, I investigate how state–society relations have been conceptualized in recent Anglophone scholarship on the post-Soviet states. Finally, I suggest that the blurring or dissolution of the boundary between the state and other aspects of society might usefully be understood in terms of the concept of "stateness" as an immanent presence in modern societies whose actualization in diverse practices gives rise to the appearance of what are called state–society relations.

CONCEPTUALIZING "SOCIETY" AND "STATE"

Debates about "state–society relations" frequently run the risk of generating considerable confusion because of the multiple (but often closely related) meanings of the two terms "state" and "society." I will consider "society" first. "Society" derives from the Latin word *societas*, meaning partnership, fellowship, or alliance, and which in turn comes from *socius*, meaning sharing, comrade, or companion. It appeared in Old French in the 12th[th] century, and its first recorded uses in English were in the 16th century, when it connoted companionship. The earliest meanings of "society" thus refer to the condition of living in association. Counterterms for these meanings might include "individual," "living in isolation," or even "loneliness," but not "state."

According to *The Oxford English Dictionary*, in the 17th century "society"[7] began to take on the additional meanings of an "aggregate of persons living together in a more or less ordered community" and "a collection of individuals composing a community or living under the same organization or government." Understood in these different ways, "society" has been variously treated as a synonym for "state," as a larger whole of which the state is one part, or as something distinct from the state. The different usages will become clearer when we consider different meanings of the term "state."

These historical developments in the meaning of the word "society" are reflected in two contrasting contemporary uses of the term. The first is more substantive and refers to a specific set of individuals, groups, and institutions, as in the phrase "British society comprises many ethnic groups." This usage is determinate, particularistic, and reifying in that it typically identifies one specific society and treats it as an entity—"this society," "our society," "Russian society," and so on. The second, which reflects the earlier meaning of "society" as the condition of living in association, is indeterminate and universalistic and invokes ideas of cohesion, integration, and unity. For example, the Human Rights Campaign (HRC) in the United

States is an organization that advocates equal rights for lesbian, gay, bisexual, and transgender people, including the right to get married. The HRC website reports that opponents of same-sex marriage have claimed that such unions would bring about "the end of society as we know it."[8] For its part, the HRC argues the opposite—that allowing same-sex couples to marry would make "society stronger and more stable."[9] These uses of the term "society" function normatively. In the HRC example, what might be termed "society-ness" is given a positive value (by both the supporters and the opponents of same-sex marriage). By contrast, Margaret Thatcher took a famously negative view: "There is no such thing as society."[10] We might say that "society" as the condition of living in association is virtual, and becomes actual in the complex assemblages of individuals and institutions that we identity as "British society," "Russian society," and so on.

Within Western political thought, we can also distinguish between two main meanings of the word "state." One, which is associated particularly with classical political theory, defines the state as an ordered or organized human community. The other, which is characteristic of much modern political theory, defines the state as an apparatus of rule or government. In the first case, the idea of "state" actually comes close to that of "society" in *The Oxford English Dictionary*'s sense of an "aggregate of persons living together in a more or less ordered community." For Aristotle, the state (polis) is, like the household and the village, "an association"[11] and an "aggregate of citizens."[12] However, it differs from and has "natural priority over" both the household and the individual.[13] According to Aristotle, "among all men … there is a natural impulse toward this kind of association."[14] With the formation of the state, he writes, "self-sufficiency has been reached, and while the state came about as a means of securing life itself, it continues in being to secure the good life."[15]

In contract theory, epitomized in the work of Hobbes, Locke, and Rousseau, the state is treated as a synonym for "civilized society," and is contrasted with the uncivilized "state of nature." In *The Social Contract*, Rousseau sets out the idea that the state comprises the people and is not separate from them. For Rousseau, the social compact

> creates a moral and collective body.... This public person, so formed by the union of all other persons, formerly took the name of *city*, and now takes that of *Republic* or *body politic*; it is called by its

members *State* when passive, *Sovereign* when active, and *Power* when compared with others like itself. Those who are associated in it take collectively the name of *people*, and severally are called *citizens*, as sharing in the sovereign power, and *subjects*, as being under the laws of the State.[16]

However, as Rousseau points out, in a remark that still rings true today, "these terms are often confused and taken one for another."[17]

Since Rousseau's time, the idea of "the state" has become increasingly detached from the idea of "the people." This change has been associated particularly with the development of the concept of civil society. Mary Kaldor writes that

> for seventeenth- and eighteenth-century thinkers, civil society was defined in contrast to the state of nature. Civil society was society characterized by the rule of law, based on certain fundamental individual rights, which was enforced by a political authority also subject to the rule of law. Indeed there was no clear distinction at that time between civil society and the state. Rather, civil society was a generic term for a secular constitutional order.[18]

By the late 18th century this had begun to change, with a "shift from civil society defined in contrast to the state of nature to civil society defined in contrast to the state."[19]

This shift had begun with Hegel, who broke with social contract theory. Hegel certainly understood the state as a political community and an ethical entity, rather than as a set of institutions. However, in *Philosophy of Right*, published in 1821, he made a distinction between three moments of social existence: the family, civil society, and the state. For Hegel, civil society was bourgeois society (*bürgerliche Gesellschaft*) and was the arena of market exchange. (Since Hegel's time, this has changed again, with civil society often defined today as an intermediate realm between the state and the private sphere of the economy.) Another difference between Hegel's conception and typical modern usage is his inclusion of the police and the administration of justice within civil society, rather than within the state, where we would usually locate them today.

More recently, as Mary Kaldor notes, at least three other meanings have become current. What Kaldor calls the "activist version" equates civil society with active citizenship, participation, and the radicalization of democracy. The "neoliberal version" understands civil society in terms of the development of voluntary associations, the third sector, and NGOs, which are increasingly engaged in the provision of services from which the state has withdrawn. By contrast, the "postmodern version" moves away from universalism. It emphasizes pluralism and the possibility of incivility as well as civility, and criticizes other concepts of civil society for their Eurocentrism.[20]

The association of the concept of "state" with the apparatus of government can be attributed in part to Marx and Engels, who suggested, in an oft-quoted phrase in *The Communist Manifesto*, that "the executive of the modern State is but a committee for managing the common affairs of the whole bourgeoisie."[21] In fact, the phrase is often misquoted to imply that it is the state (as a whole), rather than its executive, that should be considered as no more than a committee. This common misquotation further promotes the view of the state as a distinctive institution. Other forms of radical thought also represent the state as separate from society. The famous anarchist call to "smash the state," for example, implies that the state is apart from the rest of society.

In the Western intellectual tradition, the 20th century saw the emergence of the social sciences as distinctive fields of study, and the institutionalization of divisions between the different social scientific disciplines. Economics, political science, and sociology became professionalized, and the boundaries between them were increasingly policed. Each discipline required its own special object of study: "the economy" for economics, "government" or "the state" for political science, and "society" for sociology. It is no coincidence that the development of the very idea of "an economy" or "a society," and the emergence of the assumption that these labels referred to real phenomena, was associated with the establishment of economics and sociology as subjects of university study.[22]

The case of political science is slightly different. Understood as a process rather than an entity, the concept of government has a long history. *The Oxford English Dictionary* dates the oldest usage in English of "govern" in the sense of "rule with authority" to 1297, and of "government" to ca. 1566.[23] However, it was predominantly in the late 17th century and 18th century that the word "government" took on its common modern meaning in English of "the institutions charged with governing." Intriguingly, whereas economics made "the economy" its central concept and sociology presented itself as the scientific study of "society," political science eschewed the apparently analogous concept of "the polity" in favor of "government" or "the state." And on those occasions when it laid claim to politics as its principal focus, the term was used mostly to refer to the formal political process involving elections, organized interest groups, and the activities of government institutions. Thus, the rise of modern Western (especially Anglophone) social science has been the story of the separation of the disciplines and the conceptual separation of their objects of study.

It has also been the story of the "nationalization" of those objects. By "nationalization" I mean the tendency to identify different aspects of social life ever more closely with the territorially circumscribed nation-state. The rise of nationalism and the strengthening of nation-states during the 19th century were closely interrelated with the development of concepts such as "the British economy," "American society," and "the French state (or government)." These changes also coincided with the rise of positivism within the social sciences and a drawing back from metaphysical and conceptual issues in favor of empirical studies of objectively delineated entities. One result of this was an increasing tendency to define both "the state" and "society" as empirical objects rather than philosophical or ethical principles or moments.

The tendency of modern social science to nationalize its objects of study has given us the commonsense map of nationally defined entities that provides the subject matter of comparative sociology: German society, Russian society, Polish society, and so on. These units may be methodologically convenient, but they are not unproblematic. As post-Soviet experience shows, international borders can change overnight, whereas societies evolve slowly. If one takes at face value the equation of "a society" with "the population of an independent nation-state," then with the demise of the Soviet Union, "Soviet society" was apparently instantly replaced with "Ukrainian society," "Latvian society," "Uzbek society," and the rest. Yet it seems safe to assume that, for the most part, the social relations that constitute these novel entities will have remained largely intact, at least for some time. More generally, globalization has undermined the rigid division of the world into national societies. Migration, diasporic affiliations, multinational institutions, transnational social movements, global faith communities, digital communications, and a host of other social and technological changes are disrupting the neat parceling of the world into discrete "societies" as never before. Globalization has not led, though, to a unified, homogeneous "global society," but rather has produced new geographies of division and affiliation that cut across existing boundaries.

The political geographer Peter Taylor has argued that social science should adopt what he calls the "single society assumption."[24] This is the idea that, although the world is far from homogeneous, it should be regarded as a single unit for analytical purposes. Political differentiation (e.g., into nation-states) is then one of a number of intersecting forms of differentiation that generate distinct but intersecting geographies. Nation-states, although enormously powerful, should not be seen as providing a foundational spatial grid to which all other social phenomena should be expected to conform.

To summarize, if we are to clarify the nature of state–society relations, we need first to recognize the complexity of the terms "state" and "society." There are two relevant definitions of "state" ("an organized community" and "the apparatus of government") and three of "society" ("the condition of living in association," "an ordered community," and "an aggregate of individuals living under the same government"). Combining these different meanings of "state" and "society" produces six contrasting outcomes (see Table 1.1).

Table 1.1
State and Society Combined

		State as ...	
		an organized human community	the apparatus of government
Society as ...	the condition of living in association	State is the full expression of society.	State is a partial expression of society.
	an organized community	State and society are congruent.	State is a part of society.
	an aggregate of individuals under one government	Society is a part of the state.	State and society are separate entities.

THE STATE AS AN ORGANIZATION

The equation of the idea of "state" with that of "society" persists in general usage today. A 2007 article on Zimbabwe in Britain's *Guardian* newspaper is illustrative. The headline was "The Wasteland—Inside Mugabe's Crumbling State." However, the article focused not just on the problems of the Zimbabwean government but on the wider concern that the "nation" and the "country" were "sliding into chaos."[25] On the other hand, within Anglophone academic discourse the dominant trend has been from the top left of Table 1.1 to the bottom right, reflecting the rise of empiricism and positivism and the tendency to treat the objects of social scientific inquiry as substantive entities that can be demarcated and measured. This outcome has, I think, been deeply problematic, and has produced a series of rather sterile debates about how state and society are related. There is, however, a range of alternative perspectives on which we can draw to rethink state–society relations along more productive and less restrictive lines.

The 20th-century narrowing of the concept of the state to refer to the apparatus of government is apparent from the opening pages of one of the few textbooks devoted to the subject. Although published more than 20 years ago, *Theories of the State,* by Patrick Dunleavy and Brendan O'Leary, remains a useful (and widely used) account of how different theoretical perspectives have dealt with the origins, development, politics, and crises of the modern state. My purpose here is not to dispute Dunleavy and O'Leary's description of the various theories of the state they discuss in their book. Rather, I am using their account of how the state should be defined to exemplify the way in which mainstream social science deals with the question of definition.

They start with the proposition that the state is an abstraction.[26] They then suggest that there are two broad approaches to defining the state: organizational and functional. "Organizational definitions," they assert, "regard the state as a set of governmental institutions, of relatively recent historical origin."[27] Among other things, a modern state is "a recognizably separate institution or set of institutions, so differentiated from the rest of its society as to create identifiable public and private spheres."[28] Dunleavy and O'Leary acknowledge that "this approach leaves open the question of whether the state should be treated as a single unified actor, or as the sum total of the roles and activities of the individuals in state organizations, or as a conglomerate of sub-organizations."[29] Functional definitions identify the state as the set of institutions that either has particular objectives or produces particular consequences, such as maintaining social order.[30] According to Dunleavy and O'Leary, functional definitions "invariably conceptualize the state as a unitary 'actor,'"[31] although that seems to me to be debatable. They are, however, right to stress that functional approaches leave open the question of which specific institutions fall within the definition of the state. From this perspective, any organization whose goals, purposes, or effects overlap with state functions "automatically becomes part of the state."[32]

Dunleavy and O'Leary adopt the organizational definition of the state as their default definition in the remainder of the book. In doing so, they follow mainstream social scientific convention, which assumes that objects of inquiry, such as the state, can be defined prior to, and separately from, their conceptualization. The mode of reasoning is that social objects preexist our theorization of them and that we apply a process of theorization to preconstituted entities. "Theory" then becomes a process of accounting for the attributes of one set of preconstituted entities in terms of those of others. I want to suggest, by contrast, that "the state" does not exist outside and separate from human conceptualizations of it. Rather, our conceptualizations are themselves part of the becoming of the state.

Seen in this light, the contrast between organizational and functional definitions that Dunleavy and O'Leary identify may be more apparent than real. In one sense, the functional approaches they outline are not opposed to the organizational approaches. Rather, they simply provide a different way of identifying which institutions and activities make up the state. Organizational definitions limit the list to the formal institutions of government, whereas functional definitions are agnostic as to which of the vast range of human institutions "function" as part of the state and which do not. Both approaches, at least as Dunleavy and O'Leary describe them, treat the state as a set of institutions.

The frequent misquotation of Marx and Engels' reference in 1888 to the state executive as a committee for managing the affairs of the bourgeoisie may have exacerbated the tendency to define the state narrowly in institutional terms, but in general, organizational definitions of the state are most often associated with the analyses of Max Weber. He sets out the "primary formal characteristics of the modern state" as follows:

It possesses an administrative and legal order subject to change by legislation, to which the organized activities of the administrative staff, which are also controlled by regulations, are oriented. This system of order claims binding authority, not only over the members of the state, the citizens, most of whom have obtained membership by birth, but also to a very large extent over all action taking place in the area of its jurisdiction. It is thus a compulsory organization with a territorial basis. Furthermore, today, the use of force is regarded as legitimate only so far as it is either permitted by the state or prescribed by it.... The claim of the modern state to monopolize the use of force is as essential to it as its character of compulsory jurisdiction and of continuous operation.[33]

Among state theorists, most attention has been devoted to Weber's suggestion that the state is an organization that claims a monopoly on the legitimate use of force. The implications of seeing the state as an organization in the first place have been given less attention. In fact, there is a slippage in the above quotation from seeing the state as a "system of order" (i.e., as organized) to seeing it as an organization. The German term that Weber uses here is "*ein Verband*" (which translates as "organization" in the sense of a group or association) rather than, for example, "*eine Einteilung*" (which translates as "organization" in the sense of an arrangement or an ordering). At the same time, Weber's reference to the citizens as "members of the state" shows that he did not conceptualize the state as separate from society.

Weber sees the state as an organization that should be distinguished in terms of its distinctive means (the monopoly on force) rather than any particular ends, objectives, or functions. Indeed, approaches that seek to identify state institutions empirically through a description of their functions or activities are problematic. In practice, it is impossible to identify any functions that belong exclusively to the state. Somewhere, sometime, any given state activity has been, or could be, undertaken by some other organization, as Weber emphasizes.[34] For example, we might be tempted to suggest that the state comprises the judiciary; the armed forces; the institutions of government (the legislature and the executive); social, welfare, health, and education services; and so on. This conceptualization seems straightforward but presents several difficulties. Many organizations are not intrinsically part of the state, but only contingently so. For example, state hospitals exist in some countries and not in others. State schools may be common today, but were unknown 200 years ago.

The boundary between "state" and "nonstate" is thus hopelessly blurred. Numerous institutions and practices cross what is conventionally understood as the boundary of the state. Some are explicitly designed to do so: the ostensible purpose of elected legislatures is to translate attitudes, norms, preferences, wishes, needs, and desires from "the general public" into state decision making. In some areas of state activity, there is profound—and perhaps necessary—ambiguity about whether an individual's actions constitute action by the state or not. Barristers (attorneys) operate private businesses and may represent a private organization or individual, but they are also officers of the court, and thus constituent parts of the state apparatus. A doctor in a state hospital may seem like a more clear-cut case, but doctors also typically enter into professional obligations that require them to place the interests of their patients ahead of other concerns. These and many similar aporias undermine any attempt to demarcate rigidly the institutional scope of the state.

Since the 1980s, many countries have seen considerable growth of private-sector involvement in public services. Privatization can take a number of forms. Some services may be fully privatized so that they are no longer provided by state organizations at all. In other cases, governments may contract out certain activities to other operators. The private sector may also provide capital assets (through leasing arrangements), management services (such as accountancy, strategic advice, information technology support, or payroll administration), or staffing (through recruitment agencies), or it may own and operate a business whose revenue comes wholly or partly from public funds (e.g., a bus company that is paid to run buses on otherwise uneconomic routes). Today, even apparently core state activities such as incarcerating prisoners and fighting wars are undertaken by private contractors, and public goods from drinking water to the regulation of air traffic are supplied by nonstate organizations.

The reverse also applies: private and nonprofit organizations depend in numerous ways on the state. They benefit from state-supplied education, skills training, and health care, which contribute to the effectiveness of labor power. State infrastructure provision from roads to sewerage underpins the activities of most private companies. The legislative and judicial institutions of the state approve and enforce laws that provide a stable framework for business. All of this makes it impossible to neatly categorize any organization as either "state" or "nonstate." In practice, most organizations are state/nonstate hybrids.

Despite these practical problems of distinguishing typologically between state and nonstate organizations, many academic and popular discussions continue to treat the state as a separate institutional realm. Moreover, the state is routinely posited as an agent and accorded quasi-personhood. This can easily be confirmed by typing "the state" followed by any one of dozens of verbs into an Internet search engine—try "the state eats," for example! Examples of this kind of reification have appeared across the spectrum of social theory, in, for example, Marxist, feminist, and anarchist writings, as well as Weberian accounts. Reification is as apparent in calls to "take over" or "smash" the state and in arguments that the state is an "instrument" of class (or gender) domination as it is in the liberal assertion that the state acts as a neutral arbiter in social conflicts, or the conservative doctrine that the state should be protected from external or internal threats.

Reification emphasizes the state's unity, coherence, and functionality. In practice, the diverse ensemble of institutions we call the modern state is so large and complex that no one individual or group can exercise authority over the whole, and it is impossible for either to act with even the appearance of a single mind or unified purpose, whatever the rhetoric of state elites.

Reification also underpins what might be called the "separate spheres assumption."[35] This is the idea that the state constitutes or occupies a distinct segment of the social whole that then affects or interacts with other spheres, such as the economy, civil society, or the private realm.

As we have seen, the concept of "civil society" has a complex history. Today, though, it is generally understood as a realm of social action separate from the state, as Antony Giddens suggests:

> All states—as state apparatuses—can be differentiated from the wider societies of which they are part. What is "outside" the scope of the state has, since the Enlightenment, been understood in varying senses as "civil society."[36]

This supposed separation has the following features, which together form a kind of imagined geography of society. First, civil society and other segments of the social whole (such as "economy," "private sphere," and "lifeworld") tend to be treated as unified totalities. Second, the segments are bounded, so that the constituent elements of each are assumed to be—in principle, if not always in practice—specific to the segment concerned. Thus, the prison system is part of the state, businesses are part of the economy, and family life is part of the private sphere. We have already seen that this is unsatisfactory. Third, the separate spheres interact with each other (the state regulates the economy, economic activities affect family life, and so on). Fourth, these interactions are treated as external relations; that is, they are considered to be relations between preconstituted entities, rather than the processes through which such entities come into being in the first place.

Giddens, for one, finds this kind of thinking untenable, at least for modern states, arguing that

> with the rise of the modern state, and its culmination in the nation-state, "civil society" in this sense [of something separate from the state] simply disappears. What is "outside" the scope of the administrative reach of the state apparatus cannot be understood as institutions which remain unabsorbed by the state.[37]

Giddens argues that this view is consistent with the older Hegelian understanding of civil society, "for Hegel sees that 'civil society,' as *bürgerliche Gesellschaft*, is in substantial part created by the (modern) state or, put more accurately, that the two come into existence in conjunction with one another."[38] This is an important corrective to some currently popular development discourses that argue for the promotion of the institutions of civil society precisely because they are supposedly separate from, independent of, and a counter to the state.

In public discourse, the state is said variously to regulate the economy, to promote development, to undertake social engineering, to threaten (or to protect) our liberties, to wage war, to detect and punish crime, and much else besides. Sometimes the sphere of the state is viewed as an object that needs to be controlled or reduced or strengthened, depending on one's political beliefs. Either way, the idea that the state forms a separate sphere is both widespread and frequently taken for granted.

This has a number of implications. First, the separate spheres assumption paradoxically accords stateness both too much and too little importance in social life. By ascribing coherence, unity, and organization to the state, it represents the state as powerful and potentially threatening. Yet by demarcating the state as separate from society, it risks underestimating the extent to which the nominally non-state areas of social life are, in fact, permeated by state relations. Second, the separate spheres assumption reinforces the idea that politics is a special field of activity and that everyday life, civil society, and economic relationships are somehow "not political." Third, it licenses a quantitative view of the state (the state is seen as an object that is capable of growth or decline) that tends to reduce political debate to a question of whether the state should be bigger or smaller, or whether it should be "rolled back."[39] Finally, the separate spheres assumption promotes political passivity, both in the sense that the state can be treated as a machine for solving social and economic problems without requiring any effort on citizens' part, and in the sense that insofar as the state is seen as a problem, it is too large, well organized, and powerful for citizens to influence.

The rise of organizational definitions of the state and the embedding of the separate spheres assumption in public discourse arguably provide the conditions of possibility for the very concept of "state–society relations." This is because the idea of "state–society relations" makes the most sense if "state" and "society" are understood as separate (and probably preconstituted) entities that interact. The treatment of the state–society distinction was the subject of an important critique in 1991 by Timothy Mitchell.[40] He focused in particular on American political science, which, he suggested, responded to the "difficulty in drawing the boundaries of the state" in two different ways.[41] "The first," he stated, "was to abandon the state as a concept too vague and too narrow to be the basis of a general science of politics, replacing it most frequently with the concept of the political system."[42] However, according to Mitchell,

> the change in vocabulary failed to solve the problem. The boundaries of the political system, where its edges meet those of the social or other systems, proved, if anything, even more elusive than the boundary of the state.[43]

The second set of responses, advocated by Theda Skocpol, Eric Nordlinger, and Stephen Krasner, was to "bring the state back in" to political analysis.[44] Skocpol, for example, argued for treating the state (understood as an autonomous organization in it own right) as a central actor in the French, Russian, and Chinese revolutions. But these "statist" approaches, Mitchell argued,

> face a common problem and respond similarly. The problem ... is that the edges of the state are uncertain; societal elements seem to penetrate it on all sides, and the resulting boundary between state and society is difficult to determine. [Statist approaches] respond by giving the state a narrow definition, personified as a policy-making actor. Like personhood, statehood is conceived in fundamentally idealist terms. The state stands apart from society as a set of original intentions or preferences, just as persons are thought of as units of autonomous consciousness and desire distinct from their material or social world. However uncertain its edges, the state, like the person, is an essential unity.[45]

According to Mitchell, the image of the unity of the state makes it impossible for the statist approaches to understand how wider social differences influence conflicts within the state apparatus.[46] Mitchell's own approach offers an alternative. For him,

> the boundary of the state *never marks a real exterior*. The line between state and society is not the perimeter of an intrinsic entity, which can be thought of as a free-standing object or actor. It is a line drawn internally, *within* the network of institutional mechanisms through which a certain social and political order is maintained.[47]

Mitchell concludes his account by arguing that the state should be analyzed as a "structural effect," that is, "it should be examined not as an actual structure, but as the powerful, metaphysical effect of practices that make such structures appear to exist."[48]

A somewhat similar approach has been developed by Joel Migdal, one that he refers to as "state-in-society."[49] Migdal defines the state as a field of power marked by the use and threat of violence and shaped by (1) *the image of a coherent, controlling organization in a territory, which is representative of the people bounded by that territory*, and (2) *the actual practices of its multiple parts*.[50]

Both Mitchell and Migdal combine the idea that the state appears to exist as a coherent organization or structure with an emphasis on the practices that produce and reproduce that appearance or image. A focus on practices has also been central to my own account of the prosaic geographies of stateness in contemporary Britain.[51] I will return to the idea of stateness at the end of the chapter, but will first consider how debates about state–society relations have influenced accounts of post-socialist politics.

STATE–SOCIETY RELATIONS IN POST-SOCIALISM

The dynamics of state–society relations in post-Soviet Russia are discussed by political scientist Erik Hoffman in his contribution to a collection of essays titled, *Can Democracy Take Root in Post-Soviet Russia? Explorations in State–Society Relations*.[52] In his analysis, Hoffman uses the categories of "state" and "society" in line with conventional political science, and his approach has not been obviously influenced by the kind of critique advanced by Mitchell (although Migdal's "state-in-society" approach gets a brief mention). Hoffman asserts that he does "not wish to endorse any definition of 'state' or "society,'" but then goes on to "use 'state' and 'society' mostly in reference to particular 'state institutions' (e.g., cabinets, courts, and armies) and 'social institutions' (e.g., banks, schools, and churches), not state functions or activities and social forces or strata."[53] This means that while he recognizes that "the distinction between state and society should not be overdrawn,"[54] Hoffman treats "state" and "society" very much as separate spheres that interact, even likening interactions between a state and its society to "interactions between two states."[55] He implies that this is in line with Russian terminology:

> The Russian state is a *territorially delineated legal entity*, but national state (*gosudarstvennye*) institutions are not limited to those of the "Government" (*Pravitelstvo*).[56]

He further observes that

> the Russian concept of "society" (*obshchestvo*) now rivals its Western counterparts for elasticity and vagueness. But it is not just a residual category. It connotes an organization, group, or stratum that is "nonstate."[57]

If Hoffman is correct, then the Russian terminology reinforces the view of state and society as separate entities. On the other hand, he writes,

> *gosudarstvennost* is a sociopsychological phenomenon—collective and individual characterizations of Russia's physical and spiritual essence and assessments of its accomplishments and potentials—and it is not to be confused with the political institutions of the state or the officials of the current government.[58]

Moreover, Hoffman finds that the experience of post-socialism in Russia defies conventional notions of state–society relations.

> State–society relations are hard to describe, let alone explain, when a highly centralized one-party system suddenly fragments, many of its national and regional leaders place parochial and personal interests above the survival of the polity, most of its nationalized industrial enterprises are privatized, and its ethnic and non-ethnic administrative units are given tax collecting authority by the country's top politician. State and social institutions become tangled as their functions and roles intermix. State and society are considerably blurred when government ministers sell off large chunks of valuable state property at bargain prices to their favorite businessmen or bankers, who compete murderously (literally and figuratively) with other coalitions of political officials and private entrepreneurs. State and society overlap further when all of these major coalitions buy or control the major banks and mass media, with prominent businessmen shuttling in and out of government service or seeking election as legislators to gain immunity from anticipated criminal prosecution. And state and society become indistinguishable—even Kafkaesque—when most government

bureaucrats don two hats, public and private, and most public agencies double as privatized cooperatives.[59]

Hoffman recognizes that, as well as making life extremely difficult for ordinary Russians, these features of post-Soviet reality challenge established conceptualizations of state and society, and of their interrelations. In the end, though, his analysis remains rooted in the established categories of political science developed in the context of Western liberal democracy. That context then inevitably acts as the benchmark against which post-Soviet progress in the direction of democracy is measured; hence the title of the book in which Hoffman's contribution appears: *Can Democracy Take Root in Post-Soviet Russia?*

Hoffman's account is constrained by his attempt to shoehorn the empirical novelty of the post-Soviet experience into the conceptual categories of mainstream American political science. By contrast, Neil Robinson's study of the *longue durée* of the development of the Russian state under tsarism, communism, and post-socialism is more innovative. Robinson also recognizes the difficulty of providing an unambiguous definition of the state, in part because "states are defined by political factors and phenomena that are often unstable and contested."[60] His arguments are not framed explicitly as an investigation of "state–society relations." However, he does draw on Michael Mann's notion of the infrastructural power of the state, which emphasizes the penetration of state authority into a wide range of social relationships and its extension across a large spatial area. Robinson argues that state formations can be classified by their regime type (constitutional or absolutist) and by their form of administrative organization (patrimonial or bureaucratic). This analysis produces four possible state types, each with a distinct set of characteristics: constitutional-bureaucratic (the modern West), absolutist-patrimonial (tsarist Russia), absolutist-bureaucratic (the Soviet Union), and constitutional-patrimonial, which is "an unstable type of state formation … whose evolution to the constitutional-bureaucratic type is not guaranteed."[61] For Robinson, it is this unstable fourth type to which the contemporary post-socialist Russian state most closely corresponds.

Unlike Hoffman and the other contributors to *Can Democracy Take Root in Post-Soviet Russia?*, Robinson does not view the post-socialist Russian state through the normative lens of democratization theory, although his perspective is normative in other respects. The "constitutional-bureaucratic" state is presented as a desirable goal, since "states with infrastructural power have high capacity because bureaucratic impersonalism creates organizational integrity, and because social resources can be drawn upon to ensure policy implementation and the regulation of the bureaucracy."[62] Moreover,

> the relatively effective operation of a constitutional division of powers between representative legislatures and governments facilitates a particular form of embedded state autonomy. Political decisions are seen as the product of neutral processes of decision making that all society has an equal influence over, and autonomy is embedded because the state is not distanced from the society that it represents internationally and in whose name it undertakes domestic governance.[63]

It is certainly hard to argue with such a goal when faced with state practices that are routinely seen as both arbitrary and ineffective. Yet the problem is that this description represents, at best, a highly idealized depiction of the character of even Western states. In many Western countries, political decisions are not widely regarded as neutral processes over which all society has an equal influence,; nor do state bureaucracies in the West always enjoy organizational integrity. Numerous mundane (and some spectacular) state failures in established Western democracies suggest poor correspondence between actual state practices and abstract models.

Marcia Weigle's 2003 monograph on Russia's liberal project is subtitled *State–Society Relations in the Transition from Communism.*[64] Weigle's account is predicated on a central foundational assumption, namely, that the "attempt to consolidate democracy in post-Soviet Russia [is] part of a single project to institutionalize the foundations of political liberalism."[65] Political liberalism is defined here in ideal-typical terms as a normative goal. Achieving the goal requires both a set of basic principles (such as the protection of civil liberties and private-property rights and the rule of law) and the establishment of appropriate institutional and procedural mechanisms to give effect to them. The key mechanisms in Weigle's model are private property, political parties, representative democracy, an active civil society characterized by the "spirit of association," and a regulated and politically neutral bureaucracy.[66] This model is explicitly broader than economic liberalism (and neo-liberalism) with their emphasis on market mechanisms for the allocation of resources. In contrast to economic liberalism, Weigle places particular emphasis on the role of civil society (in its modern rather than Hegelian sense) and on the relations among civil society, political society, and the state.

Weigle identifies a paradox that forms a central component of her narrative. After an initial period in the late 1980s and early 1990s when there was an upsurge of grassroots civic mobilization, post-Soviet Russia experienced the growing dominance of elites and what Boris Kagarlitsky has called the "smothering of civil society."[67] The paradox is that since this "smothering," the project of political liberalism has had to rely on state elites and state institutions to drive it forward, even though political liberalism is supposed to involve only a very limited role for the state and is firmly opposed to state-driven social change.

Russia's Liberal Project does acknowledge that the early post-Soviet "bottom-up" push toward the development of an autonomous civil society and political liberalism gave way to elite domination and a growing authoritarianism. Given this, it is not clear why (apart from her normative commitment) Weigle sees the liberal project as the fundamental dynamic shaping the direction of post-Soviet state–society relations. There seems to be much stronger evidence (even in the pre-Putin period covered by Neil Robinson's book) for Robinson's "constitutional-patrimonial" regime or something like an "authoritarian-statist" project.

Robinson's characterization of constitutional patrimonialism also resonates with Richard Sakwa's analysis of state and society in post-communist Russia.[68] Sakwa observes that the question of the state has been relatively neglected in post-communist studies, in part because it is sometimes assumed that strong state institutions are one of the legacies of communism. In fact, though, "the late communist state exhibited the classic feature of a weak state, succumbing to societal and clientalist pressures, and increasingly unable to impose its authority on public and private actors."[69]

This means that one of the tasks facing many post-socialist states is the reconstitution of state institutions themselves. The state is thus both object and agent in the process of "transition." Sakwa emphasizes the weakness of the Russian state, but suggests that this "in part reflects the pathologies of Russian society" and specifically "the inability of civil society to structure and sustain a hierarchy of political preferences, either vis-à-vis the state or economic management."[70] Nevertheless, he suggests that there has been some development of civil society,[71] further observing that "the development of a civil society that could sustain and interrogate the logic of a market economy is perhaps the greatest challenge facing post-communist societies."[72]

Earlier in the present chapter it was seen how Timothy Mitchell's definition of the state as a structural effect draws attention to the appearance of the existence of a state–society boundary.[73] Political liberalism depends on the rigorous maintenance of this apparent boundary. However, Sakwa's work reveals just how blurred this boundary has become:

> In Russian we have the peculiar situation in which the institutions of both state and civil society are gelatinous, but in which something has emerged at the margins of the visible range of the social science spectrum, a distinctive form of quasi-society combining pre-modern forms of social solidarity and postmodern hyper-individualism.[74]

Sakwa adds that

> post-communist civil society, however, has not only a normative but also a pathological aspect.... In places coalitions of organized crime and former members of the nomenklatura have forged a new ruling class. Organized crime has begun to provide some of the services that citizens expect of the state, for example, security, protection of commercial business, mediation in disputes and contract enforcement.[75]

Sakwa not only emphasizes the social and political novelty of many aspects of state–society relations under post-socialism, he also recognizes the need for conceptual innovation to describe and account adequately for the new.

Conceptual innovation is the hallmark of Andrew Wilson's approach to post-Soviet politics set out in *Virtual Politics: Faking Democracy in the Post-Soviet World*.[76] Wilson eschews idealized conceptions of democratization in favor of a warts-and-all account of the machinations, manipulations, and brazen deceptions that characterize political life in Russia, Ukraine, and most of the other former Soviet republics. Wilson argues that post-Soviet politics is virtual in two senses. First, many politicians, political parties, and policy platforms are invented and covertly promoted by state and economic elites. For example, in some cases fake opposition groups have been set up by the incumbent ruling elite in order to legitimize its subsequent election victory as democratic, while minimizing the risk that a real opposition rooted in civil society will emerge. The process of invention is enabled by a network of public-relations agencies, political consultants, fixers, and agents, many of whom have no ideological or political commitments but are available for hire to the highest bidder. Politics is also virtual in a second sense: that it takes place largely in the media and in particular on television. Incumbent elites frequently control media outlets, and their public-relations agencies ensure the careful choreographing and stage-managing of events and performances for maximum televisual effect.[77]

While some of these features of virtuality (especially in relation to the media) are present in contemporary politics in the West, Wilson insists that the post-Soviet version is highly distinctive. To varying degrees, post-Soviet states meet four key conditions for the practice of virtual politics: a powerful but amoral elite, a passive electorate, a culture of information control, and a lack of an external counterpoint (i.e., Western indifference).[78]

Wilson concedes that the image of "vibrant pluralism" associated with the 1988–1991 period that Weigle links to bottom-up liberalism may have some truth in it.[79] Nevertheless, virtuality predominates, with the result being a sharp dislocation between the world of politics and the mass of the population:

> Post-Soviet virtuality is ... a radically top-down phenomenon, unlike in the West, where politicians are now often overwhelmed by a plethora of new media and messages over which they have no control. Given the Soviet legacy of highly formalized, ritualized political participation, a true political society, "those core institutions of a democratic political society—political parties, elections, electoral rules, political leadership, interparty alliances, and legislatures—by which society constitutes itself politically to select and monitor democratic government," has yet to emerge, resulting in a "demobilisation of the social" that is more radical than anything yet seen in the West.[80]

If the political system (of parties, elections, and other components of liberal democracy) is virtual and radically disembedded, what of the state? "Russians," Wilson writes, "are used to venerating the state, but also to placing it at a distance, on a pedestal. They are therefore also used to an indistinct image of power and to coping with the plasticity or viscosity of power."[81] This observation resonates with Sakwa's comment about the gelatinous character of both the state and civil society. Although Wilson does not offer a theory of the state as such, the implications of virtual politics for our understanding of the state and state–society relations are profound. Whereas *Virtual Politics* reveals a radical separation between state elites and society (understood here as the majority of the population), it also shows that the inevitably porous boundaries between state institutions and political elites on the one hand, and private economic interests and organized crime on the other, have largely collapsed. Whatever may be their purchase elsewhere, theories of the state that treat it as a separate sphere or a bounded entity certainly seem unlikely to aid understanding of post-Soviet circumstances.

CONCLUSION: IMMANENT STATENESS

What appears to be needed is a way of talking about the qualities that are associated with "the state as a structural effect" without reverting either to an organizational definition that risks positing the state as an entity or to a functional definition that tends to ignore the heterogeneity and internally contradictory character of the state apparatus.

I have suggested elsewhere[82] that that the concept of "stateness" is a useful way of grasping these qualities. "Stateness" refers to an idea that is expressed in French with the word *étaticité* and in German as *Staatlichkeit*. As I conceive it, "stateness" is an aspect of most social relations and processes to a greater or lesser degree (some social relations are highly "statized," while others are not). It refers to those aspects of a given social process that invoke, imply, or depend on the idea of the state. Thus, to some extent "stateness" can be thought of in a similar way to other conceptual categories, such as "gender." As feminists have long argued, "gender" is not a distinct area of social life that can be understood in isolation. Rather, all social relations should be seen in gendered terms, and gender refers not to essential biological differences between men and women but to human understandings of the implications of those differences. In a similar vein,

I want to suggest that stateness is an immanent presence in social life, but one that is actualized or effectuated in specific circumstances. Stateness is thus a qualitative attribute of social relations; it is something that we carry with us in our bodies (and in our embodied minds), and which we express (or perhaps sometimes suppress) in our actions and behavior. In a sense, it is we who give life and existence to the state: the state is our performance.

Of course, "stateness" is not the only aspect of social life that works in this way. Familial ties, ethnic and religious identities, professional expertise, creativity, desire, physical abilities, and other aspects of social life travel with us and are realized and performed in individual behavior and social interactions. Clearly, some societies are more "statized" than others, but stateness varies in intensity within individual nation-states too. If we give life to the state through our interactions, we do not do so equally in all contexts. My actions actualize stateness most strongly when I file my tax return, vote in an election, or write to my elected representative; to a lesser extent when I teach my students in a public university subject to considerable state regulation; and rather weakly when I take my children to the cinema. However, even in this last case stateness is present to some extent: in the film classifications that determine what my children can watch, in the planning regulations that influence where the cinema can be built, in the tax incentives made available by the government to encourage the national film industry, in the provision of a national electricity network that provides the power for the projector, and so on.

While stateness may be a pervasive presence in the lives of almost all modern humans, other qualities pervade the actors and institutions we conventionally think of as making up the state. Thus, state institutions and practices are necessarily gendered, for example. Similarly, ethnicity, kinship relations, knowledge and beliefs, and economic considerations all inhere in the minds and bodies of those who people the state apparatus and find expression in these individuals' actions and relationships. Just as stateness permeates the parts of society conventionally defined as outside and separate from the state, so state institutions are suffused with the life outside.

A number of benefits flow from rethinking "state–society relations" in terms of varying intensities of stateness. This approach draws attention to the actual social practices through which the state in actualized, and to the labor involved in producing the effect of the state, and provides scope to think about whether stateness (including in so-called mature democracies) should sometimes be seen as fragmented, incomplete, prone to failure, and fragile. At the same time, it recognizes that the state is present in a much wider range of social relations and processes than is allowed for by the conventional separation of social objects into the domains of economics, sociology, and political science. It emphasizes the uneven development of states between, but also within, countries. It may reveal that the reach of the infrastructurally strong modern (Western) state may be less comprehensive and geographically even than writers such as Michael Mann and Antony Giddens suggest.[83]

Finally, a key theme emerging from an approach that stresses the varying intensities of stateness is the active production, regulation, and transgression of the boundaries among the state, the private sphere, and civil society. Immanent stateness permeates social relations of all kinds, albeit unevenly. But stateness is only actualized—made effective—in particular conjunctures or assemblages. It is these actualizations that establish, for a time, the "proper" boundary between the state and other parts of society. But that boundary is not natural or permanent. Rather, it is subject to constant contestation. It is thus constantly policed and regulated—both by the state and by institutions of civil society—and constantly transgressed, so that it becomes blurred, or breaks down entirely, or moves its position. "State," "society," and the relationships among them are not universal, stable, or uncontested, but contingent, mutable, and themselves the products of situated social and material practices.

NOTES

1   Vladimir Shlapentokh, "Hobbes and Locke at Odds in Putin's Russia," *Europe-Asia Studies* 55 (2003): 983–84.
2   Ibid., 984.
3   Ibid.
4   Ibid., 985.
5   Francis Fukuyama, *State-Building: Governance and World Order in the Twenty-First Century* (London: Profile, 2004), 25.
6   Ibid., 28.
7   "society, n,." Oxford English DictionaryED Online,. June 2010,. Oxford University Press (available at . 20 Aug. 2010 http://dictionary.oed.com/cgi/entry/50229768, accessed August 20, 2010).
8   "Why Are 'Pro-Family' Groups Attacking These Families," Human Rights Campaign (2007), (available at www.hrc.org/millionformarriage/hrc_adcenter/).
9   "The Goodridge Family," Human Rights Campaign (2007), (available at www.hrc.org/millionformarriage/hrc_adcenter/goodridges.html).
10 Margaret Thatcher Foundation, Interview for *Woman's Own* ("no such thing as society"), September 23, 1987 (available at http://www.margaretthatcher.org/document/106689, accessed August 20, 2010).
11 Aristotle, *The Politics*, section 1252a.
12 Aristotle, *The Politics*, section 1274b. For Aristotle, a citizen is one who participates "in giving judgment and in holding office" *(The Politics*, 1275a).
13 Ibid., section 1253a.
14 Ibid.
15 Ibid., section 1252b.
16 Jean-Jacques Rousseau, *The Social Contract* (London: J. M. Dent & Sons, 1913 [1762]), 15–16, emphasis in the original.
17 Ibid., 16.
18 Mary Kaldor, *Global Civil Society: An Answer to War* (Cambridge, England: Polity Press, 2003), 17.
19 Ibid., 18.
20 Ibid., 8–9.
21 Karl Marx and Friedrich Engels, *The Communist Manifesto* (London: Penguin Books, 2002 [1888]), 221.
22 On the emergence of the idea of "the economy" as a separate sphere, see Timothy Mitchell, *Rule of Experts: Egypt, Technopolitics, Modernity* (Los Angeles: University of California Press, 2002), 80–119.
23 "govern, v.," The Oxford English Dictionary,. 2nd ed., 1989,. OED Online,. Oxford University Press. (available at 20 Aug. 2010 http://dictionary.oed.com/cgi/entry/50097290, accessed August 20, 2010).
24 Peter J. Taylor, *Political Geography: World-economy, Nation-state and Locality* (Harlow: Longman, 1989), 4.
25 "The Wasteland—Inside Mugabe's Crumbling State," *The Guardian* (London), March 17, 2007.
26 Patrick Dunleavy and Brendan O'Leary, *Theories of the State: The Politics of Liberal Democracy* (London: Macmillan, 1987), 1.
27 Ibid.
28 Ibid., 2.

29 Ibid.
30 Ibid., 3.
31 Ibid., 4.
32 Ibid., 3.
33 Max Weber, *Economy and Society: An Outline of Interpretive Sociology* (New York: Bedminster Press, 1968), 56.
34 Ibid., 55.
35 Joe Painter, "State: Society," in *Spaces of Geographical Thought: Deconstructing Human Geography's Binaries*, eds. Paul Cloke and Ron Johnston (London: Sage, 2005).
36 Anthony Giddens, *The Nation-State and Violence* (Cambridge, England: Polity Press, 1985), 20.
37 Ibid., 21–22.
38 Ibid., 21.
39 Cf. Philip O'Neill's account of the "qualitative state": Philip M. O'Neill, "Bringing the Qualitative State Iinto Economic Geography," in *Geographies of Economies*, eds. Roger Lee and Jane Wills (London: Arnold, 1997).
40 Timothy Mitchell, "The Limits of the State: Beyond Statist Approaches and Their Critics," *American Political Science Review* 85, no. 1 (1991): 77–96.
41 Ibid., 77.
42 Ibid.
43 Ibid.
44 Peter Evans, Dietrich Rueschemeyer, and Theda Skocpol, eds., *Bringing the State Back In* (Cambridge, England: Cambridge University Press, 1985); Stephen D. Krasner, *Defending the National Interest: Raw Materials Investments and U.S. Foreign Policy* (Princeton, NJ: Princeton University Press, 1978); Eric Nordlinger, *On the Autonomy of the Democratic State* (Cambridge, MA: Harvard University Press, 1981); Theda Skocpol, *States and Social Revolutions: A Comparative Analysis of France, Russia, and China* (Cambridge, England: Cambridge University Press, 1979). For another critique of calls to "bring the state back in" to political analysis, see Bob Jessop, "Bringing the State Back In (Yet Again): Reviews, Revisions, Rejections, and Redirections," *International Review of Sociology* 11, no. 2 (2001): 149–73.
45 Mitchell, "The Limits of the State," 88.
46 Ibid.
47 Ibid., 90, emphasis in the original.
48 Ibid., 94. Mitchell distinguishes this claim from the structural account of the state developed by Nicos Poulantzas. See Nicos Poulantzas, *Political Power and Social Classes* (London: New Left Books, 1973), and Nicos Poulantzas, *State, Power, Socialism* (London: New Left Books, 1978).
49 Joel S. Migdal, *State in Society: Studying How States and Societies Transform and Constitute One Another* (Cambridge, England: Cambridge University Press, 2001).
50 Ibid., 15–16, emphasis in the original.
51 Joe Painter, "Prosaic Geographies of Stateness," *Political Geography* 25, no. 7 (2006): 752–74.
52 Erik P. Hoffman, "The Dynamics of State-SocietyState–Society Relations in Post-Soviet Russia," in *Can Democracy Take Root in Post-Soviet Russia? Explorations in State-SocietyState–Society Relations*, eds. Harry Eckstein, Frederic J. Fleron Jr., Erik P. Hoffman, and William M. Reisinger (Lanham, MD: Rowman & Littlefield, 1998).
53 Ibid., 71.
54 Ibid., 74.

55   Ibid., 73.
56   Ibid., 78, emphasis added.
57   Ibid., 79.
58   Ibid., 82.
59   Ibid., 82–83.
60   Neil Robinson, *Russia: A State of Uncertainty* (London: Routledge, 2002), 3.
61   Ibid., 6.
62   Ibid., 165.
63   Ibid.
64   Marcia A. Weigle, *Russia's Liberal Project: State–Society Relations in the Transition From Communism* (University Park: Pennsylvania State University Press, 2000).
65   Ibid., 1.
66   Marcia A. Weigle, *Russia's Liberal Project: State-SocietyState–Society Relations in the Transition Ffrom Communism* (University Park, PA: Pennsylvania State University Press, 2000), 6-–12.
67   Boris Kagarlitsky, *The Disintegration of the Monolith* (London: Verso, 1992).
68   Richard Sakwa, "State and Society in Post-Communist Russia," in *Institutions and Political Change in Russia*, ed. Neil Robinson (Basingstoke, England: Macmillan, 2000).
69   Ibid., 194.
70   Ibid., 203.
71   Ibid., 205.
72   Ibid., 207.
73   Mitchell, "The Limits of the State."

74   Sakwa, "State and Society," 207.
75   Ibid., 208.
76   Andrew Wilson, *Virtual Politics: Faking Democracy in the Post-Soviet World* (New Haven, CT: Yale University Press, 2005).
77   Ibid., 33–35.
78   Ibid., 47.
79   Ibid., 32.
80   Ibid., 48.
81   Ibid., 35.
82   Joe Painter, "Prosaic Geographies of Stateness," *Political Geography* 25, no. 7 (2006): 752–74.
83   Giddens, *The Nation-State and Violence;* Michael Mann, "The Autonomous Power of the State: Its Origins, Mechanisms and Results," *Archives Européennes de Sociologie* 25 (1984): 185–213.

CHAPTER 2
POST-SOVIET POWER IN ANTHROPOLOGICAL PERSPECTIVE

NIKOLAY N. KRADIN

Anthropological theories of state formation have developed generally separate theories from those in the field of political science, although anthropologists acquainted with the works of the modern political scientists can discover many common features in the mechanisms of the establishment of historical and modern political institutions. When the widely known works of Robert Michels[1] concerning the social-democratic parties of West Europe in the 20th century are considered, it is suggested that social practices have varied little since the first chiefdoms of Sumer and Egypt.

Michels shows that any political party or trade union organization faces various challenges in the course of its activities (e.g., the organization of political campaigns and elections, publishing activity, contract negotiations). These activities take a lot of time, and sometimes demand special training. If the organization has a large membership, then additional efforts are necessary to coordinate these activities. Little by little, managerial machinery is created to provide vital services to the organization, such as collecting dues and interacting with other organizations.

Functionaries concentrate in their hands the organizational infrastructure, organs of the press, and financial assets. If an opposition emerges within the organization, then all of these instruments can be used against the revisionists. Over the course of time, as the financial position and status of leaders attain stability, their psychology undergoes a similar change. They may aspire now to maintain their own stability rather than fulfilling the programmatic aims of their party/organization. Therein, Michels says, lies "the iron law of oligarchy."[2] But let us replace some variables in Michels' picture. For example, envision a group of neighboring villages instead of the trade union or party cell, gifts and tribute instead of dues, and a chief instead of a party organizer. One then obtains a typical picture of how the chiefdom developed into the early state. Yet for all of this, we are still focused on a key issue: why this form of state formation (i.e., oligarchic) is not new to post-Soviet Russia and other states of the Commonwealth of Independent States (CIS).

To what degree do the mechanisms for establishing power structures differ between historical (or ancient) and modern societies? Political anthropology helps us to understand that modern politics is rooted in the past, and particular forms of social order can be traced to ancient human communities. Political anthropology is also of great importance in understanding political processes in modern societies that are moving toward a democratic system of national government.

In the present chapter, I focus on providing a historical perspective on the character of institutions of power and political processes in Russian society, focusing on how they are in many respects *traditional* (to use Max Weber's terminology). I argue that combining aspects of traditional societies with the direct and uncritical adoption of Western liberal values can produce surprising results that are the opposite of what was intended. The multiparty system can be expressed in the formation of party structures on a clan-tribal or confessional basis, and also may result in large-scale interethnic or religious conflicts. The separation of powers in democratic societies can result in chaos and disorder (because the separation of powers is, in essence, not characteristic of traditional societies), and then the establishment of a military junta, and other developments that further undermine representative rule.

Today's situation in the former Soviet republics clearly demonstrates the limits of the classical models of social and political science developed with exclusive reliance on Western materials. For many years, volunteers from Western Europe and the United States have heartily preached to Russian businesspeople, economists, and lawyers about the correct way to form a market economy. However, instead of privatization and a civilized market, Russia has experienced the appropriation of resources by people in high positions. Instead of a "normal" market, I term the current situation a pseudo-market mafia economic infrastructure. The State Duma, the government, and the president have issued one normative document after another, but economic and political actors ignore these pronouncements because, in Russia, there is little respect for laws (or the rule of law) as does exist in other European countries. In Russia, a directive or an order, such as the so-called telephone law—indeed, anything else—has always been the deciding factor, rather than the constitution and laws. Telephone law is a special form of politics in Russia. Consultations by telephone between political leaders, as well as telephoned directives, are more important than the written law. (It will suffice to note the manner in which the Russian government executes the budget adopted by the State Duma.)

BUREAUCRATIC CHANGE AND INDIGENOUS SOCIAL PRACTICE

In compiling the extensive experience of problem solving in the traditional and colonial societies of Asia, Africa, the Americas, and the Pacific, political anthropologists have shown that the traditional and bureaucratic patterns of domination (in the Weberian sense) are difficult to render compatible in practice. Democracy is the voluntary integration of independent individuals. In post-traditional societies, an individual is a part of a single whole (tribe, clan, fraternal association); hence, all of his or her activity is mediated by this single whole. In such societies (in the more general context of all non-Western societies), features identified by Weber such as rationality, depersonalization, and competence are not characteristic.[3]

Over the course of time, anthropologists have come to understand that the formal abolition of traditional power institutions (a practice characteristic of states with a socialist orientation), and appointment of petty officers from that segment of the resident population that had received a European education did not, for the most part, produce the desired result—in other words, making someone be the responsible party. The former chiefs reserved a high status for themselves, while appointees from the nonprivileged groups, especially outside groups, had, as a rule, no prestige.

Pressure exerted by the rational bureaucratism introduced by colonizers has resulted in the deformation and, even in some places, the destruction of the traditional model of power, its desacralization, and the establishment of a temporary system of power. In many formerly traditional societies (especially in Africa), a dual political culture is established in which traditional forms of power are present in parallel with the official administrative bodies. The particular interdependency is traced between the position of an individual in the party-state machinery and his status in the men's union or secret society. Advancement up the hierarchy in one system is, as a rule, accompanied by a rise in status in the other; quite often, leaders of the traditional system of hierarchy not directly present in the official structure of political power do have a profound impact on the most important political decisions. Moreover, as the parallel structures often exert a greater effect on their supporters than the state does in traditional societies, these structures directly influence the character, forms, and pace of the evolution of democracy. Therefore, the prospects for stable democratization in Africa depend on whether the African governments will come to an agreement with these authoritative social forces on a mutually acceptable and efficacious mechanism for the separation of powers and responsibility and the fair distribution of material resources to the benefit of all.[4]

In the society with strong clan and tribal relations, the scale of this phenomenon becomes very large. It is related to the fact that the bearer of power in the traditional society always acts not by himself but as a representative or the leader of the particular group. He is understood to be at the group's center, the concentration of the sacred force, and should share with the group his power functions and privileges. Therefore, it is not surprising that in countries of the Third World and the newly independent states of the former Soviet Union, the ruling elite is making efforts to displace from positions of responsibility all those who are not connected to the members of these groups by blood, family, or other ties.

THE ETHNOTERRITORIAL ROLE IN STATE FORMATION

In colonial and postcolonial societies, the absence of a coincidence between the administrative-territorial divisions and boundaries and those of the territories of residence of traditional tribal structures is a characteristic that often causes acute ethnonational and intergovernmental disputes. In recently independent former colonies that preserve their traditional tribal structure, party structures are often formed on a clan-tribal or confessional basis or as a tool of the personal influence of one or another leader. In this situation, there are often no political and ideological differences between the programs of different parties. Under such conditions, elections to the representative bodies of power are based on tribal affiliation or principles rather than on political programs. On the whole, all of this produces instability in the ruling coalitions: they are often changed, there is acute factional struggle, and there is no political stability in the society.[5]

In much of the former Soviet Union, especially in the national republics (the newly independent states as well as a number of subject jurisdictions of the Russian Federation), the role of the clan and tribal remnants has been prominent and can be useful in forecasting political processes (Kradin, 2000). The situation in Russia since 2000 has remained practically unchanged. It is period of political conservatism and new turn bureaucratization. Nearly all of the hypotheses I advanced in my 2000 article have been realized, with the exception of the latest developments in Kyrgyzstan and recent declarations by the leaders of Kazakhstan and Turkmenistan about future presidential elections in their states.

As an example of the anthropological analysis, any Asian state of the CIS can serve where parties and movements that arose in the years of perestroika and after the Soviet collapse were established on an ethnic basis. Summarizing an investigation of post-Soviet nationalism, Anatoly M. Khazanov has concluded that the scheme of international relations within the post-Soviet space did not change, and national *nomenklatura* in most of the newly independent states replaced the Russian *nomenklatura*. At that, the ethnic Russians, having no ties with the *nomenklatura*, became the minority group, with all the dubious amenities of this ethnosocial status.[6]

Unfortunately, sociological inquiries often cannot adequately reflect the existing situation. Direct formulation of the question "Do you prefer that the leader be your relative?" or "If you were a leader, would you gather all your relatives near yourself?" results, as a rule, in unambiguously negative answers.[7] Under certain conditions, people are often likely to assess themselves in an unduly positive way. However, different indirect data indicate the presence of certain manifestations of ethnic discrimination.

Kazakhs, for example, are inclined much less than other nationalities to note the presence in their country of interethnic conflict, violations of human rights, bureaucratic abuses, and discrimination in the case of nominations to executive positions. In addition, they believe more often that the titular nationality should have certain advantages over other ethnic groups in Kazakhstan (in matters such as education and privatization). What is especially symptomatic is that more than a third of Kazakhs think that these preferences should be taken into account in elections to positions of authority.[8]

It is evident that all of this has been caused by the presence of the powerful traditional stratum in the mentality (including the political culture) of Kazakhs. Practically all non-Kazakh respondents note among the characteristic features of the Kazakh ethnicity "hospitality," "traditionalism," and "respect for relatives."[9] The best example of Kazakh "traditionalism" is the custom of mutual aid within the clan or tribe, and, as a particular variant of this, protectionism with respect to relatives.

The fact of the ethnic inequality of rights is more truly reflected in the number of representatives of one or other nationality in the different authorities. Consider again the example of Kazakhstan. During 1990–1993, the ethnic composition of the supreme legislative body of the country approximately corresponded to that of the republic population. The coefficient of the ethnic representation[10] of the titular population was 1.2. It was 0.9 for Russians. At the same time, a share of the Russian population in the executive bodies was much less. At the local level, the coefficient for Russians decreased by 1993–1994 from 1.0 to 0.7, while for Kazakhs it increased from 1.2 to 1.3. The proportion of Kazakhs in the government bureaucracy was also much greater: the coefficient for Russians was 0.6, while that for Kazakhs was 1.5. The situation became even more aggravated over the course of the 15-year period.[11]

A similar state of affairs is characteristic not only of the recently independent states but also of multiethnic subject jurisdictions of the Russian Federation. So, for example, in Sakha (Yakutiya), the coefficient of representation was 1.8 for Yakuts and 0.6 for Russians.[12] In Tatarstan, the designation *nation* (i.e., as applied to Tatars) prevails in both the administrative machinery and the parliament. (The coefficients are 1.6 and 1.5, respectively.[13]) In Bashkortostan, the coefficient of representation for legislative power is equal to 1.9 to 2.5 for Bashkirs, 0.5 to 1.0 for Tatars, and 0.5 for Russians; the coefficients for executive power are 2.7 to 3.0 (Bashkirs), 0.5 to 0.7 (Tatars), and 0.4 to 0.5 (Russians).[14] One could give many similar examples.

However, this opposition has not only an international basis (i.e., titular nationality against Russians), but also an intraethnic basis. At present, one can trace the influence of the local clan and clan-tribal groups in each of the now independent Central Asian states of the CIS, as well as in the multinational republics of Russia. This phenomenon in Soviet anthropological thought has been described by different terms, *mestnichestvo, ulusizm,* and *kumovstvo* (tribalism or tribal nationalism), and is considered a remnant of the clan-tribal or patriarchal-feudal order. For example, the Soviet party functionaries regarded it as serious even after the establishment of Soviet power over the entire territory of the country. One head of the Communist Party organization in the Kalmyk District even wrote, in 1926:

> The *ulusizm* makes itself evident in the fact that every Soviet Communist Party member defending his *ulus* with respect to all party and Soviet questions reaches such a point that he forgets any party discipline proclaiming a principle: without regard to if my country is right or not, but it is my country and I am obliged to defend it. It is a most serious disease, hindering the work not only of the local party organizations but also of the governing body itself.[15]

At the same time, many people in Kazakhstan assumed that the intraparty struggle in the center had developed between the clans of Lenin and Trotsky.

After the political repressions of the 1930s, *ulusizm* was temporarily forgotten, although it has persisted to the present, with anthropologists' studies of the Soviet political system demonstrating its presence in Central Asia and the Caucasus. In the years of perestroika, publications on this subject again appeared in the mass media. It turns out that the question of *ulusizm* as applied to the power problem remains as urgent as it was about 70 years ago.

However, in real situations, all is much more complex. In the broadest sense, the phenomenon is a playing out of the protectionist impulse of members of government to bring aboard next of kin, distant relatives, and compatriots, with this practice being accompanied by the dismissal from key posts of people not related to the hierarch. It would be foolish to claim that such practices had been eliminated in industrial societies. Rather, this is a widely distributed evolutionary phenomenon with deep biological roots: opposition between one's group and a foreign group, and real preference for contact with relatives. Protectionism with respect to relatives is a particular aspect of so-called personal relations in the preindustrial, traditional society. In the industrial society, each person is present as a detached individual, while relations between people take the form of commodity-money ties. In preindustrial social systems, each person appears as an element of any stable collective (e.g., community, clan, military-hierarchical organization), and relations between people are personal rather than physical. The situation is one of personal coercion and power as applied to relations of inequality and domination.[16]

The practice of personal relations is founded on important theoretical grounds. According to Max Weber, in the traditional society,

> the place of firm business competence is occupied by the competition of initially given by the master at a free discretion, then becoming long-term and, finally, stereotyped commissions and powers. They produce the competition for due chances for the payment of made efforts of both special messengers and masters themselves: owing to such interests, the business competences and, thereby, existence of departments are often constructed. All of special messengers having the long-term competence are, first of all, the court functionaries of the master; the competence *not* related to the court (extrapatrimonial) is given to them on the basis of a quite superficial business similarity of the activity field in their court service or on the basis of, mainly, quite arbitrary choice of the master.[17]

Hence, all activity in similar political structures is based on personal relations, even personal devotion. (In this regard, one should keep in mind the developments of autumn 1998 to summer 1999, a period of seemingly endless reshuffling of the Russian Federation government.)

The phenomenon of government based on personal relations is pervasive in societies with strong clan and tribal ties. This is related to the fact that the power bearer in traditional society acts not by himself but as the representative and leader of a particular group. He is perceived as its center, the focal point of the sacred force, and should share with it his imperial functions and privileges. It is not accidental that it is not the particular ruler but the whole of his lineage or clan that is considered to possess the "mandate of heaven" for the rule of one territory or another, as it was in the empire of Genghis Khan and his heirs. (This is especially true with respect to the Central Asian states.) Therefore, it is not surprising that in the countries of the Third World and the recently independent states of the former Soviet space, the ruling elite is making efforts to remove from responsible posts all who are not connected with members of these groupings by blood, family, and other ties.

The official insularity of the staffing policy of the party-governmental *nomenklatura* is conducive to such removals. So, for example, accession to the post of first secretary of the Communist Party of the Azerbaijan Soviet Socialist Republic by Heydar Aliyev resulted in the gradual removal of the protégés of his predecessor, Veli Akhundov, and penetration of the republic's governing bodies by Aliyev's compatriots from the enclave of Nakhichevan. After Aliyev moved to Moscow to take a promotion to a national-level position, a new rotation of cadres began in Azerbaijan with the arrival of a new party secretary, Kyamron Bagirov. A similar process occurred in the party-governmental *nomenklatura* in the Uzbek Soviet Socialist Republic during the reign of Sharaf Rashidov. On occasion, information on the clan character of government bodies in the Central Asian and Transcaucasian republics has infiltrated to news media bodies. For instance, in Georgia in 1973, a change in the *nomenklatura* elite became public knowledge when the official party newspaper, *Zarya Vostoka* (in an article published February 28, 1973), made it apparent, at least by inference, that a plenum of the Central Committee of the Communist Party of Georgia had taken place:

> Favoritism, regionalism, *zemlyachestvo* [friendly association of persons from the same area], and position hunting prosper owing to kindred ties and corruption.... Wives and members of the family begin to substitute for their husbands of high standing in positions, and state problems begin to be solved in the narrow kindred, family, and friendship circles.
>
> Officials were commissioned on the basis of patronage, string pulling, kindred ties—by a principle of personal devotion rather than on their professional and moral qualities...
>
> Sometimes, unworthy persons were appointed to the top posts.... These words were often heard: "Master said so," "Master wishes so."

Among the leading employees, a strong opinion on the undesirability of airing dirty linen in public was cultivated. The facts of bribe taking and theft were kept secret. Indeed, thanks to media censorship, the actual extent of corruption is underestimated.

At present, in each of the former Soviet republics of Central Asia, the influence of local clan and clan-tribal groups remains a tradition. In Uzbekistan, such groups concentrate on the basis of geography (in the cities of Toshkent, Buxoro, and Samarqand). In terms of numbers, the metropolitan clan predominates. Taking an administrative post is only possible if one belongs to one or another clan. The access of minority groups (especially Russians) to the prestigious institutes of higher education has been closed.

In Kyrgyzstan, there are several levels of the traditional elite structure that were not destroyed as a result of the technological and cultural modernization carried out during the Soviet period. Modernization "only weakened but did not liquidate the established—in the course of centuries—hierarchy of subordination and co-subordination of tribes and clans, their struggle for influence and power."[18] At the highest level of the hierarchy, the elite is subdivided into two adversarial groupings of natives of the southern and northern regions of Kyrgyzstan, with general domination by the northern natives. The origins of this confrontation are rooted in the two-wing system of the traditional genealogical organization of nomads. The dual division of the political elite is complicated by the presence of a number of authoritative clan groups. Among the northerners, these include, for example, the clans of Tugu (from the region around the lake Issyk-Kul), Salto (from the Chuiskaya Valley), and, especially, Sary-Bagy (found in the Chuiskaya Valley and the Narinskaya Region), which claims among its sons the man who was president of Kyrgyzstan during its transition to independence, Askar Akayev.

Beyond that point, there is a tendency for the activation of the representatives of the former aristocratic clans (*manapsky*) driven from the power and control mechanisms during the period of Soviet power.[19] They take an active part in the struggle for influence at the local level, attempt to move their protégés into positions of control or other key posts in different branches of the power machinery, and make efforts to remove the "non–well-born" party-governmental *nomenklatura* who climbed the ladder during the years of Soviet power.[20]

In Tajikistan, clan divisions can be traced in several ways, first of all, along a line from the "northern" Leninabad District, the most urbanized in the country, to the agricultural "south." The Leninabad group (the Khudzhandsky clan) traditionally has been one of the most authoritative formations. In Soviet times, its representatives held key party-governmental posts in the republic. This tradition remains in post-Soviet times. Rakhman Nabiyev, who was president of Tajikistan when it became an independent state, came from the Khudzhandsky clan.

The Kulyab clan represents the interests of the residents of the agricultural regions of the south. After coming to power in 1992, a member of this clan, Imomali Rahmonov, effected the gradual removal of representatives of Leninabad from key posts in state security bodies, law enforcement agencies, ideological institutions, and other organs of the government.

Geographically and politically, the Gissar community is located between Leninabad and Kulyab. This Gamar group's interests are concentrated in trade and consumer cooperatives. The Islamic party of revival and extremist groups of soldiers (*vakhabits*) comes from this group. The particular place is occupied by Pamirs' people (Badakhshan grouping), who speak East Iranian languages and are Shiites-Ismaelites, unlike most Tajiks who are Sunnis. Some refer to this community as a small Tajik "Sicily" (consider the theoretical basis of specificity of the political system of mountain people).[21]

Questions concerning Kazakhstan's political structure are more frequently studied. In the ethnic consciousness of Kazakhs, four levels are identified: (1) ethnic-national, (2) *zhuz* (tribal or chiefdom confederation), (3) clan-tribal, and (4) territorial, which is independent of ethnic identity. Local (clan) structure is based on the *zhuz* genealogy (Great, Middle, and Small Horde). The Great Horde *zhuz* traditionally has roamed the Semirechye (Seven Rivers) area of what is now southeastern Kazakhstan. The Middle Horde *zhuz* has occupied eastern Kazakhstan. The Small Horde *zhuz* has located in western Kazakhstan. However, the privileged clans—the descendants of Genghis Khan (the Tope) and the descendants of saints (the Tozha)—were ranked genealogically above any of the other *zhuzes*.[22]

The northern Kazakhs, as a rule, know the name of their *zhuz* and their tribal group of the lower taxonomic level. In the south, this information is of more essential significance because on this, the status and financial position of an individual depend. (This was especially true under the conditions of the shortage economy under socialism.) The elder generation at a marriage carries out the exogamy principle. Clan divisions can be traced in funeral rites. For example, when burying the deceased, the bereaved family is expected to give presents to the patriarchs of all clan groups residing in the settlement.[23]

The well-known Kazakhstan anthropologist and opposition political leader Nurbulat Masanov has considered in detail the history of the struggle among the clan groupings of Kazakhstan in the 20th century.[24] In Soviet times, in spite of the cruel Stalinist repression, the representatives of the Middle Horde *zhuz* dominated the Kazakh intellectual elite for a long time: in the arts, in the sciences (its members included many academicians and even presidents of the Academy of Sciences of the Kazakh Soviet Socialist Republic), and, to a lesser extent, in the party-state machinery. Since the 1960s, the leading positions have been taken by the Elder *zhuz* or Great Horde. Its first member promoted to a prominent administrative position was the leading Kazakh poet Dzhambul. (Dzhambul has only one name given his status as a traditional nomad.) Dinmukhamed Kunayev, who held the post of first secretary of the Communist Party of Kazakhstan from 1962 to 1986, was from the Elder *zhuz*. Making use of personal contacts and the patronage of Soviet leader Leonid Brezhnev, Kunayev gradually appointed his fellow tribesmen and relatives to many key posts, including his younger brother, who became the president of the Academy of Sciences of the Kazakh Soviet Socialist Republic. During Kunayev's long tenure as first secretary, future president Nursultan Nazarbayev started his own political career. In the years of Kunayev's reign, Kazakhs were recruited into the party-state machinery at all levels. By 1989, they made up 51 percent of the administrative personnel, even though they accounted for only 3 percent of the qualified workers and 11.3 percent of the unqualified workers in the republic. By 1994, the disproportion had become even more extreme, with the share of Kazakhs in the president's administration and ministry reaching 74 percent. The disparity between Kazakhs and Russians in favor of the former is present even in the local administrations of the northern areas, where the proportion of Russians is traditionally higher.

This tendency continues to intensify. Only the elections to the Supreme Soviet approximately reflect the actual demographic proportions of nations and ethnic groups.[25]

The Younger *zhuz* (Small Horde or clan) traditionally has played a secondary role. This *zhuz*'s status as the lowest-ranking horde in Kazakhstan has had the effect of unifying its members. During the administration of Yuri Andropov, the Soviet leader possibly considered the promoted workers as competitors with Brezhnev's party elite, and appointed them to a number of the key posts. However, the death of Andropov after only a brief period in office and the restoration of Brezhnev's system hindered this process.

In the years of perestroika, the rivalry among the *zhuzes* recommenced. In response, Mikhail Gorbachev decided to send to Kazakhstan a man from the outside—Gennadi Kolbin being at that time the first secretary of the Ulyanovsk Region Committee of the Communist Party of the Soviet Union. However, this appointment prompted spontaneous disorders in December 1986. Because Kolbin, in the opinion of Nurbulat Masanov, mainly considered his armchair a jumping-off place for a career in the metropolis, the coming of Dinmukhamed Kunayev's protégé Nazarbayev was simply a matter of technique.[26]

By 1989, Nazarbayev's time had arrived. Coming to power, he pensioned off all of his former and potential competitors, approved a power monopoly for the Elder *zhuz*, and, after the Soviet collapse, further consolidated the position of his clan, appointing his nearest relations to various state posts. This phenomenon grew to the point that a new term—*chemolganization* of power structures (the village of Chemolgan is Nazarbayev's hometown)—appeared in the news media. It is not also accidental that the regions of Akmola and Karaganda, to which Nazarbayev has ties dating to his childhood, trust him more than other parts of Kazakhstan.[27]

Nevertheless, a clan struggle invisible to outside observers continues to this very day. An expert inquiry done by the Institute of Kazakhstan Development showed that 29 percent of respondents believed that *zhuz* and clan affiliation played a significant part in the distribution of privileges, posts, and offices.[28] Once the members of the Kazakh Academy of Sciences (as noted above, such positions traditionally were occupied by representatives of the Middle Horde) rejected Nazarbayev's protégé

Azamat Dzholdasbekov and elected the candidate of their clan, the economist Kenjegali Sagadiyev, the destiny of the academy was predetermined: it was absorbed into the ministry (first the Ministry of Education and then the Ministry of Education and Science), where all of the highest posts were distributed from the top. The confrontation between the *zhuzes* and the backstairs, in Masanov's opinion,[29] or, rather, a dread of joining in the opposition of the Middle and Younger *zhuzes*, predetermined the cancellation of the presidential election and prolongation of the Nazarbayev regime to 2000, as well as the transfer of the national capital to Akmola. Because "the ethnic peace in Kazakhstan is very fragile and exists mainly because of the quantitative parity of the two major ethnic groups,"[30] the transfer of the national capital to the north, according to the plan of the ruling elite, was expected to contribute to migration from the south and an increase in the share of the Kazakh population in the northern regions, and, in that way, further the consolidation of the national state system. On the other hand, a movement of all key power mechanisms to the territory of the traditional residence of the Middle Horde would have the effect of further weakening opposition to the incumbent president's power.

But situations of this type exist not only in the newly independent countries of the CIS. In Russia's Kalmykia Region, about 85 percent of townspeople and more than 90 percent of the rural population identify with one or another tribal group. The struggle for power is carried out between three major tribal groupings: the Torgut, the Derbent, and a clan with more recent origins, the Buzavsk, which consists of descendants of Kalmyks from the Don River region. Similar processes can be seen in the Russian republic of Tuva, for instance, as well as in many multinational subject jurisdictions of the Russian Federation.

Ethnographic and anthropological studies have shown that the situation in Chechnya, in contrast to that of the genealogically hierarchical structures of yesterday's nomads of Kazakhstan and Kyrgyzstan, has always been of the egalitarian and decentralized type—perhaps as a result of many years of conflict. But then, mountain societies have always been distinguished by their thirst for nonhierarchical models of political organization.[31]

The Chechens have no noble class or other privileged hereditary group. They are divided along clan, territorial, and, to a certain extent, confessional lines. The Chechen *teips* (clans) survived the Soviet period and now acquire more and more influence in the political life of the society.

Devotion to one's clan remains the highest value in the Chechen mentality; feuds can last for generations. The Chechens are divided into three basic territorial groups: those who reside in the Terek River valley (they experienced a greater Russian influence than the two other groups); those who live in the foothills; and the true mountaineers (economically the poorest and, at the same time, the most traditional part of the Chechen ethnos). During the Soviet period, political power in Chechnya was held by people from the lowlands. During the rule of Dzhokhar Dudayev, the rebel leader killed by the Russians in 1996, the mountaineers were his very loyal supporters. Although all Chechens are considered Sunni Muslims, they are more accurately the followers of two different Sufi orders or congregations, Nakshbandiya and Kadyriya, which contend for influence in Chechen society. Even in the past, the Chechens were unable to unite and elect a national leader because they did not wish to give priority to one clan or territorial group over the others. Their only national leader was Sheikh Mansur, who lived in the 18th century and was the first leader of the Chechens in their war with the Russian Empire.[32]

A distortion of the basic aim of modernization is also demonstrated by the results of the direct introduction of Western liberal-democratic institutions into traditional societies. Movements to create components of modern political culture such as multiparty systems, parliamentary rule, and the separation of powers often have inverse results, very undesirable from the viewpoint of the democratization task. Political-anthropological studies reveal that party structures in post-traditional societies are quite often formed on a clan-tribal or confessional basis or as tools to advance the personal influence of one leader or another. Under such conditions, election to representative bodies is, as a rule, based on tribal or religious principles rather than on political programs. As a result, many people are induced to participate in tribal, interethnic, and interconfessional conflicts, a development that results in the instability of the ruling coalitions and the absence of political stability in general. All of this causes crises and political revolution. Events in Chechnya itself since the mid-1990s illustrate this.

In the present state of affairs, those in power see quite often that the only way to maintain stability lies in the establishment of authoritarian, single-party military regimes. It is not accidental that practically all the states in the Asian part of the CIS are characterized by autocracy.

One more feature of traditional power must be kept in mind. The separation of powers is an institution going through a long evolution of the kind, one might say, that was endured by Europe over the course of many rebellions and revolutions. By definition, this phenomenon is not characteristic of archaic and traditional societies. The ruler in a traditional society is the only bearer of the sacral status, and all other independent branches of the power are automatically perceived as undesired competitors not only by the ruler himself but also by most people. Therefore, in the post-traditional societies a political leader of the charismatic type invested with nearly plenary powers is, quite often, the governing body of both country and party. It is thus clear why most countries of the CIS followed a similar process of political transformation: dissolution of the legislative body, enactment of a constitution extending the powers of the president, and "gentle" terror with respect to the opposition and independent mass media communication.

This process can be illustrated by several examples. In 1993, in Kazakhstan, a confrontation developed between the legislative and executive powers. However, in contrast to Russia, where a similar confrontation took the form of armed conflict, in Kazakhstan the main threads of the political game were always in the president's hands. In spite of the unwillingness of the Supreme Soviet to self-destruct, an enterprising group involving the "approved" deputies was established that began to agitate for self-dismissal within the parliament. In December 1993, the parliament ceased to exist. Under the constitution of 1995, the legislative and judicial authorities were put under the executive authority (e.g., the president could now appoint judges; the constitutional court was liquidated). A referendum in 1995 prolonged the authority of President Nazarbayev to the end of the 20th century. (He continued to serve in that office in 2009.) This phenomenon received the name *bashism*, after Saparmurad Niyazov, ruler of Turkmenistan until his death in 2006 and popularly known as Turkmenbashi, who was the first leader of a Central Asian member of the CIS to begin a campaign to prolong his authority to the end of the 20th century.

In Uzbekistan, the MuslimIslam Karimov holds the posts of president of the country and head of the cabinet of ministers. The Supreme Soviet of Uzbekistan is controlled by the president. In the autumn of 1991, some of the deputies in opposition voiced criticism of the president. In response, an amendment to the law on deputy status was introduced into the Supreme Soviet, and was accepted in the summer of 1992. According to the introduced clarifications, any deputy, according to the decision of the superior legislative body of the country, could be unseated for "conduct discrediting the title of the people's deputy, making anticonstitutional actions directed toward the derogation of the state system, and destabilization of the sociopolitical situation, as well as appeal to such actions."[33] It does not require much imagination to grasp how avidly the executive branch of government would take advantage of the ambiguities in this amendment.

The constitution, as Sergei Panarin judiciously observes,[34] is mainly oriented to demonstrating the democratic structure of the young state to world opinion. It does not explain the mechanisms of presidential elections, the organization and activity of the cabinet of ministers, or registration of the public unions and movements (see Articles 56, 90, and 98). As has been noted, in 1995 the president's term in office was extended to 2000. (Like his counterpart in Kazakhstan, President Karimov also remained in office in 2009.) In the style of Soviet times, a large-scale campaign to exalt the Karimov cult was launched in the country. There is internal and external censorship in the mass media. The parties existing in the country are, per se, pro-presidential. Opposition, whether secular or religious, runs the risk of persecution.

The most unitary form of the state structure occurs in Turkmenistan. In 1992, a six-year moratorium on the multiparty system was proclaimed there, which effectively put President Niyazov beyond the control of the legislative power. All of the levers of the executive power became concentrated in his hands. He held the power to appoint and dismiss the prosecutor general and the chairmen of the Supreme Court and the Supreme Economic Court (a body that rules on disputes between private enterprises and state agencies), as well as the freedom to dissolve the People's Assembly (the national parliament) if it gave a vote of no confidence to the government he had appointed. In 2000, when Niyazov's power was at its peak, Panarin wrote:

> [N]ominally, the country is a republic with a presidential form of government. But its head has truly unlimited authority. The Turkmenbashi regime combines fantastically the features of both primitive and patriarchal rule, and it increasingly resembles the

rule of the traditional Oriental monarch, using, nevertheless, some modern techniques of power. So, on the one hand, there is comprehensive police control over the population, while on the other, populist gestures of all kinds in ... its social defense are made. The party structure is not developed absolutely; the press is semiofficial and frankly mercenary. Any criticism of the power is ignored; opposition is crushed and expelled; the few remaining *pravozashitniki* are subject to systematic intimidation and periodic court actions.[35]

Possibly the least authoritarian system of government in Central Asia is in Tajikistan. Even so, under the constitution of 1994 the president possesses a very wide range of prerogatives, although his power is in a way limited by the Supreme Assembly, which is entitled to approve all members of the cabinet of ministers and has many more important control functions. However, this "democratism" is most likely related to the struggle between different influential clans in the country and a lack of sufficient force to crush the opposition.[36]

The Russian variant differs only in one respect. While the usurpation of power in the Central Asian republics was generally achieved peacefully, President Boris Yeltsin needed tanks and armored troop carriers in October 1993. However, on the whole, the mechanism of transformational processes is practically the same. As in the other newly independent states, the state machinery swelled considerably under a constitution adopted in 1993, the president was granted the right to control the judicial authority and dismiss the legislative bodies; the institution of the office of governor-general was also characteristic. After the resignation of Yeltsin in 1999, whatever balance remained between the democratic ideals of the first president of Russia and his policies based on his former experience as party leader was broken. Yeltsin's successor, Vladimir Putin, followed other principles of rule. The tendency toward a power hierarchy and the abolition of the appointment by election of chief executives at different jurisdictional levels became even stronger. In fact, the institution of local government—one of the bases of any democracy—disappeared. The changes that consolidated legislatively the right to intervene in the affairs of individual regions and to dissolve local parliaments were introduced in the 1993 constitution. The transformation of Russia also occurred at the local level. The main components of these processes were the all-embracing role of the patrimonial power and a lack of development of the individual and civil society. All of these developments testify that, in the largest single component of the former Soviet Union (i.e., the Russian Federation), a rational bureaucratic system of power was *not* formed.

TOWARD AN EXPLANATION

Socialism can be considered a highly specific, anticapitalist variant of secondary modernization.[37] However, this modernization was carried out under extremely specific conditions. It came to an end with the establishment in the Soviet Union, and then in other countries of the socialist world, of a very specific system of power in which rational (party and bureaucracy, other institutions), personal (predominance of the individual power over the law), and charismatic (cults of the chief, father of the nation) components were present.

In the course of the collapse of socialist society, traditional ties on the ethnonational periphery escaped from the envelope of rational-bureaucratic relations. However, in post-Soviet Russia itself, a stable model of the personal system of power has been formed on account of the traditional neglect of legal institutions.

Patron–client ties occupy one of the most significant places in the aggregate of similar relations. As Mikhail Afanasyev has clearly demonstrated in a number of works,[38] such ties never completely disappear in the course of modernization and can occur not only in post-traditional societies but also in developed modern and even postmodern ones. (The mafia is the most striking example.) Patron–client relations are based on the necessity for cooperation between persons of different status under conditions of economic, social, or political instability. Persons with low status can be provided with resources and sources of subsistence, and can serve in a defensive role on the side of their patron. In this way, they fulfill particular obligations or compensate patronage by material gifts or other payments. These relations are convenient for both sides, and what is more important, they satisfy the requirements of people in regard to confidence and a sense of affiliation in the developed, industrialized society. To the societies in which traditional values are, as before, of a sufficient importance, similar circumstances are essential.

These relations are of a personal and informal nature; are based on an inequality of status, wealth, and access to resources between the patron and his clients; represent a combination of exploitation and compulsion, with voluntary gifts and services; and have externally the form of ties of mutual obligation, cooperation, and mutual interest.[39]

The character of power in post-traditional states is not too different from that in systems of traditional rule. In many respects, the influence of the political leader in post-traditional societies remains in the form of patrimonial features. This influence is based to a greater extent on patronage relationships than on rational legitimism and law. In the special literature, it has been noted time and again that the *personal* character of power in post-traditional and even developed industrial societies forms the basis of the political institutions, and relations between the patron and his clients determine political life at all levels, from the presidential palace to the crudest village.[40]

To a large extent, these conditions are caused by the traditionally important role of the state in the economic sector and, therefore, by the great role of the power-property. For this reason, administrative posts are sources of personal off-budget income (e.g., the issuance of licenses, payments for lobbying of one's interests, bribes) rather than means for the growth of status within the bureaucratic hierarchy.

In the post-traditional Asian societies, patron–client relations play a significant stabilizing role. In Montesquieu's time, it was already common practice to characterize Asian societies, in contrast to those of Europe, as purely despotic. Such a point of view has certain grounds. In fact, many of the ancient, medieval, and modern societies of Asia could be classified as regimes with an authoritarian-traditional system of rule. (The same could be said of such societies in Africa and the Americas.) However, the despotism of the superpower in the East is strongly exaggerated. The striving for uncontrolled rule is strongly suppressed there, on the one hand, by the existence on the lower level of communal, tribal, professional, and other organizations alleviating, to a certain extent, the press of power on the individual. On the other hand, in traditional cultures (including Asian ones), the paternalistic perception of the state by subjects is characteristic. For this reason, the masses never strive to change the existing regime but only demand that the heads observe justice. Finally, in Asia there have been various categories of persons (chiefs, landowners, patrons, rich peasants, headmen, etc.) and groups and associations (bureaucratic machinery, castes, clans, etc.) that have pretended to a certain percentage of power and to guarantees of their own status and property, and thereby have had the capability to be both conductors of the purposes of the supreme power and brakes on the process of change. A scholar of Indian society has noted that the impossibility of realizing evolutionary institutional reforms in India pushed a desperate Indira Gandhi to strict, unpopular measures:

> The hereditary caste groups, each of which occupied ritually the higher or lower position with respect to the others (all of them have been guided in their interrelations by standards of asymmetric rights and obligations), have formed the blocks of social organization in hundreds of thousands of Indian villages.[41]

In modern Russia, client relations—although they have a certain occurrence (in particular, in business and politics, but to a greater extent in the criminal sphere, and especially widely among the nationalities of Central Asia and the Caucasus)—do not have as much of a role as in post-traditional Asia. Personal relations are developed to a greater degree. In the administrative and managerial system of the Russian Federation, they are most conspicuous in the personal character of presidential power. The president is a supraparty figure not related to any political grouping. Under the constitution he is entitled, without consultation with anybody, to dissolve the legislative bodies and to shift the chairmen of government and key ministers. This power was clearly demonstrated in the last years of Boris Yeltsin's rule, when, guided only by personal predilections, he changed prime ministers several times in the course of a year. The government is the nonpolitical body occupied only with economic and social problems. The heads of the Ministry of Defense, Federal Security Service, Ministry of Internal Affairs, Federal Agency for Government Communications and Information, Federal Frontier Service, and so on, answer directly to the president. All of the most key decisions are elaborated in the administration of the president, a body comparable, by its functions and status, with the Central Committee of the Communist Party of Soviet days. Each subject jurisdiction of the Russian Federation has the careful attention of the eyes and ears of the president—his inspectors at the local levels. In addition to them, there are the regional representatives—so-called governors-general with their numerous mechanisms that, according to plans of the creators of this bureaucratic body, should further strengthen the vertical line of executive power. In the time of Putin, the levers of total power have been still more extended.

However, the personal character of the power of the Russian president is only the tip of the iceberg. Similar relations penetrate deeply throughout the power pyramid in Russia. One of the most competent specialists in this matter had the chance to interview, over a long period of time, functionaries of different hierarchical levels. He writes that "the most important component of today's administrative process in Russia is the clientage ties (relations of personal devotion and patronage), which (1) penetrate practically the whole machinery, (2) have a determining effect on the functionary's career, (3) determine the ways conflicts are settled, and (4) are perceived by most employees as normal, natural conditions of the machinery activity."[42]

Afanasyev's sociological inquiry, conducted among more than a hundred functionaries of the federal and regional power structures in 1995 in the Russian Academy of Public Service, shows that the representatives of the administrative elite themselves acknowledged a wide expansion of personal contacts in their environment (see Table 2.1).

Table 1
Nature of Personal Contacts among Federal and Regional Government Functionaries

Extent of ties	Family kindred ties	Zemlyachestvo ties (i.e., ties based on place of origin)	Ties among mess mates	Ties based on personal relationships
Not extensive	30%	15%	15%	5%
Occasional	55%	60%	60%	35%
Very extensive	15%	25%	25%	60%

Sources: M.N. Afanasyev, "Genesisi i Sotsialnaya Sushchnost Burokratii v SSSR" [Formation and Social Essence of Bureaucracy in the USSR] (Ph.D. diss., Moscow Public Scientific Foundation, 1989), 71; and Afanasyev, Klientism I rossiiskaya gosudarstvennost [Client Relations and the Russian State] (Moscow: MONF, 1997), Fig. 1, 227.

Table 2.1 demonstrates how embedded within personal relations the modern Russian administrative elite has become. Only about a third of respondents noted that family-kindred relations did not extend among the functionaries. The share of the other forms of personal relations is much greater. At the same time, personal devotion and patronage are most dominant. Only 5 percent of respondents said they believed that similar relations did not extend to administrative environment. Finally, there is one more interesting point. According to the respondents' opinions, the extent of the occurrence of family-kindred relations and *zemlyachestvo* in Russia was less than that of personal relationships. This assumes the important structural differences between the power system established in Russia and those of the other countries of the CIS (primarily the Central Asian states).

According to data from the same study, the main factors in the functionary's career in Russia are personal relationships and patronage. (This opinion is shared, to one extent or another, by 95 percent of respondents.) Examination of the biographies of some politicians shows that if the present-day Russian functionary does not follow the personal model of conduct and attempts to adapt his (or her) activity to the framework of management of the rational type, then his (or her) tenure most likely will be short. Such a factor as the influence of family-kindred and *zemlyachestvo* relations is also present, but its role is one order of magnitude less, though it is comparable to not-unimportant criteria of the functionary at any level, such as assiduity. A certain role in one's career is played by support of some economic structure, ethno-national affiliation, or ideological conviction. It is indicative that, in the opinion of the respondents, education and office qualifications did not influence the career of the Russian functionary of the end of the 20th century.[43]

In post-Soviet times, the number of functionaries of all levels and denominations has sharply increased. The number of generals in today's Russian army is several orders of magnitude more than in the Soviet army during the World War II. According to calculations by Mikhail Voslensky,[44] the nomenklatura in the Soviet Union accounted for about 3 million people (taking the members of families into account). The number of functionaries and their nearest relations comprised about 1 million people (0.5 percent of the population). By the turn of the 21st century, according to specialists' estimates, the number of Russian functionaries had increased several times. Their maximum number, including their families, was estimated at 7.2 (i.e., 1.8 X 4) million people. This is about 5 percent of the Russian Federation population. New measures related to the strengthening of the vertical line of power in the country resulted in one more qualitative jump in the number of functionaries. All of this has taken place against the background of the prolonged economic and political crisis, a reduction in the country's area of about a fourth, and a decrease in the population by about half.[45]

In Russia, most of the real levers of power are controlled by the same people who represented the Soviet elite. Only the deputy corps and business elite have been rotated; among these groups, a little less than half of the people are not tied by the past to the Communist Party *nomenklatura*. In the government and other higher echelons of power, only about 25 percent of persons do not have ties to the party *nomenklatura* of the past. In the regional elites, the share of such individuals is even less: 17 percent. Analysis of the age composition of the Soviet and Russian elites in the last several decades allows one to characterize the changes in the composition of the administrative elite as a "revolution of deputies," with the key posts found in the hands of the younger generation of persons from the Soviet *nomenklatura*.[46] Each Russian functionary of the top managerial level costs the treasury an average of approximately $30,000 a year. According to estimates by various analysts, about a third of the national budget is spent on maintenance of the bureaucracy.

All of this suggests that a developed democratic political system in Russia, as well as in most of the territory of the former Soviet Union, has not been created. Key components, such as the emancipation of the political individual, a stable multiparty system, and independent mass media have not been developed. (See the chapter by Olga Malinova in the present volume for a detailed discussion of the role of mass media in creating public opinion.) The authorities, as a rule, continue to be very suspicious of independent mass media, and prefer to act in a closed environment. They use different methods to put pressure on the news media, and attempt to achieve a state monopoly on television and radio broadcasting and even to control the Internet.

Numerous small parties and associations have been established to address any number of specific problems. The overwhelming majority of already-existing parties (except perhaps for communist ones) were established as tools of the personal influence of one leader or another, while in the multinational regions, the parties and movements are established on an ethnic basis. Quite often, these are the only differences between parties (even names and programs can be very similar). In politics and power structures, patron–client relations predominate.

Most political forces do not want to observe the democratic rules of play accepted in the West. The elected presidents (like chief executives at all levels in the former Soviet Union), as well as subordinate functionaries, try to get out of any restriction on their personal power and dispose of the legal opposition. However, the latter, on coming to power, acts the same way. Too much in the political culture of the CIS countries belongs to the past and is related to the traditional system of power and rule.

Will the Russians be able to overcome the burden of traditional state domination (*étatism*) and create a stable democratic society? When I first proposed this question to my colleagues in 1999, it seemed to me that my perspective was more or less optimistic. After President Yeltsin's resignation, the silencing of opposition and the acquiescence of the masses in subsequent years, my predictions became much more pessimistic. However, the Ukrainian and Kyrgyz lessons show that all our theoretical conceptions can be erroneous. In this case, I offer paradoxical ideas: naturally, as a researcher I would like my conclusions to be confirmed by future developments. But as a Russian citizen, I would like them to be proven erroneous. In this case, the answers to my questions can be given only in the course of time.

NOTES

1. R. Michels, *Political Parties* (New York: Free Press, 1968).
2. Ibid.
3. T. Cheng and B. Womack, "General Reflection on Informal Politics in East Asia," *Asian Survey* 36, no. 3 (1996): 320–37.
4. M. Owusu, "Domesticating Democracy: Culture, Civil Society, and Constitutionalism in Africa," *Comparative Studies in Society and History*, 39, no. 1 (1997): 120–52.
5. G. Balandier, *Anthropologie politique* [Political Anthropology] (Paris: Presses Universitaires de France, 1967).
6. A.M. Khazanov, *After the USSR: Ethnicity, Nationalism, and Politics in the Commonwealth of Independent States* (Madison: University of Wisconsin Press, 1995).
7. B.D. Smagambetova, "Rodoplemennoy Factor v Sisteme 'Rukovoditel-Podchinennyi'" [The Clan and Tribe Factors in the "Boss-Subordinate" System], *Sotsiologicheskie issledovniia* 3 (1998): 20–23.
8. M.M. Arenov and S.K. Kalmykov, "Etnosotsialnaia Deisivitelnost Kazakhstana"

[Ethnic and Social Reality in Kazakhstan], *Sotsiologicheskie issledovnii*a, 3 (1998): 45–58.

9   Ibid., 56, Table 8.

10   The coefficient is calculated as follows: percentage of ethnic group members in a given institution (e.g., national parliament) divided by percentage of ethnic group in total population (e.g., national population). If the coefficient is equal to 1, the ethnic group in question is proportionately represented. If the coefficient is more than 1, the ethnic group is over-represented, and when the coefficient is less than 1, the group is under-represented.

11   A.B. Galiev, et al., *Meznatsionalnye Otnosheniia v Kazakhstane: Etnocheskie Aspekty Kadrovoy Politiki* [International Relations in Kazakhstan: Ethnic Aspects of Rulers' Polity] (Almaty, Kazakhstan, 1994).

12   Khazanov, *After the USSR*.

13   M. Kh. Farukshin, "Politicheskaya Elita v Tatarstane: Vyzovy Vremeni I Trudosti Adaptatsii" [The Political Elite in Tatarstan: The Call of Time and the Difficulty of Adaptation], *Polis no.* 6 (1994): 69–79.

14   R. Gallyamov, "Politicheskie Elity Rossiiskikh Rspublik: Ocobrnnosti Transformatsii v Postsovetskii Period" [Political Elites of the Russian Republics: Features of Transformation in the Post-Soviet Period], in *Transformatsiia Rossiiskikh Regionalnykh Elit v Sravnitelnoy Perspective* [Transformation of Russian Regional Elites: Contemporary Perspectives], 163–74 (Moscow: Public Scientific Foundation, 1999).

15   I. Glukhov, *Ot Patriarkhalshchiny k Sotsializmu* [From Patriarchy to Socialism] (Astrakhan, Russia: Glukhov, 1982), p. 180.

16   M. Godelier, *The Enigma of the Gift* (Cambridge: Polity Press, 1996); M. Mauss, *The Gift* (London: Routledge, 1990 [1925]; Michels, Political Parties; M. Sahlins, *Stone Age Economics* (Chicago: Aldine, 1972).

17   Max Weber, *Wirtschaft und Gesellschaft* (Tubingen: Verlag von J.C.B.Mohr (P.Siebeck), 1922), 131–32.

18   A.M. Vasil'ev, ed., *Pistsovetskaya Tsentralnaya Asia: Poteri i Obreteniia* [Post-Soviet Central Asia: Losses and Findings] (Moscow: Vostochnaya, 1998), 296.

19   P.I. Kushner, *Gornaia Kirgiziia: Sotsiologicheskaya Razdedka* [Kyrgyzstan Mountain: Sociological Expedition] (Moscow: N.p., 1924).

20   Vasil'ev, *Pistsovetskaya Tsentralnaya Asia*.

21   Ibid., 217–19, 242–43.

22   N.E. Masanov, *Kochevaia Civilizatsiia Kazakhov* [The Nomadic Civilization of the Kazakhs] (Moscow and Almaty, Kazakhstan: Gorizont and Sotsinvest, 1995); Masanov, "Kazakhskaia Politicheskaia i Intellektualnaia Elita: Klanovaia Prinadleznost i Vnutriklanovoe Sopernichestvo" [The Kazakhstan Political and Intellectual Elite: Clan Belonging and Interethnic Rivalry], Vestnik Eurasii 1, no. 2 (1996): 46–61; Khazanov, *After the USSR*; O.B. Naumova, *Sovremennye Etnokulturnye Protsessy u Kazakhov v Mnogonatsionalnykh Raionakh Kazakhstana* [Contemporary Ethnic and Cultural Processes in Multicultural Regions of Kazakhstan] (Ph.D. diss., Institute of Ethnology and Anthropology of the Russian Academy of Sciences, Moscow, 1991); Smagambetova, "Rodoplemennoy Factor."

23   Naumova, *Sovremennye Etnokulturnye*.

24   Masanov, "Kazakhskaia Politicheskaia i Intellektualnaia Elita."

25   Galiev, *Meznatsionalnye Otnosheniia v Kazakhstane*; Khazanov, *After the USSR*.

26   Masanov, "Kazakhskaia Politicheskaia i Intellektualnaia Elita."

27   I.O. Mal'kova, "Vlast' v Zerkale Meniy Elektorata" [Authority in a Mirror of Opinions of the Electorate], *Sotsiologicheskie issledovniia* no. 3 (1998): 9–13.

28 Smagambetova, "Rodoplemennoy Factor."
29 Masanov, "Kazakhskaia Politicheskaia I Intellektualnaia Elita."
30 Khazanov, *After the USSR*, 168.
31 A.V. Korotayev, "Mountain and Democracy: An Introduction," in eds. N.N. Kradin and V.A. Lynsha, *Alternative Pathways to Early State*, 60–74 (Vladivostok, Russia: Dalnauka, 1995).
32 Khazanov, *After the USSR*. For details on the situation in Chechnya, see V.A. Tishkov, *Obshchestvo v Vooruzennom Konflikte: Etnografiia Chechenskoy Voiny* [Society in a Military Confrontation: Anthropology of the Chechen War] (Moscow: Nauka, 2001).
33 A.M. Vasil'ev, ed., *Pistsovetskaya Tsentralnaya Asia: Poteri i Obreteniia* [Post-Soviet Central Asia: Losses and Findings] (Moscow: Vostochnaya, 1998), 95.
34 Panarin, "Politicheskoe razvitie gostarstv Centralnoy Asii v svete geografii i istorii regiona" [Political Development of Central Asian States: Historical and Geographical View of Region], *Vestnik Evrasii/Acta Eurasica*, no 1 (2000): 90-132.
35 Ibid., 105.
36 Vasil'ev, ed., *Pistsovetskaya Tsentralnaya Asia*.
37 M.N. Afanasyev, "Genesisi i Sotsialnaya Sushchnost Burokratii v SSSR [Formation and Social Essence of Bureaucracy in the USSR] (Ph.D. diss., Moscow Public Scientific Foundation, 1989); A.V. Fursov, "Vostok, Zapad, Kapitalism" [Orient, West, Capitalism], in ed. V.G. Rastiannikov, *Kapitalism na Vostoke vo vtoroi polovine XX veka* [Capitalism in the East in the Second Half of the 20th Century], 16–133 (Moscow: Nauka, 1995).
38 For example, Afanasyev, *Klientism I Rossiiskaya Gosudarstvennost* [Client Relations and the Russian State] (Moscow: MONF, 1997).
39 Ibid.
40 S. Eisenstadt and L. Roniger, *Patrons, Clients, and Friends: International Relations and the Structure of Trust in Society* (Cambridge: Cambridge University Press, 1984); E. Gellner and J. Waterbury, eds., *Patrons and Clients in Mediterranean Societies* (London: Ducksworth, 1977).
41 V.G. Khoros, et al., eds., *Avtoritarism i Dempkratiia v Razvivaiushikhsia Stranakh* [Authoritarianism and Democracy in Countries of the Third World] (Moscow: Nauka, 1996), 266; Khazanov, *After the USSR*.
42 Afanasyev, *Klientism I rossiiskaya*, 233.
43 Afanasyev, *Klientism I rossiiskaya*.
44 M. Voslensky, *Nomenklatura*. (Moscow: Sovetskaya Rossiia, 1991), 91.
45 N.N. Kradin, "Elementy Tradicionnoy Vlasti v Pososovetskoy Politicheskoy Kulture: Antropologicheskiy Podkhod" [The Elements of Traditional Power in Post-Soviet Political Culture: An Anthropological Approach], in ed., E.B. Shestopal, *Obrazy Vlasti v Politicheskoy Kulture Rossii* [Images of Power in Russian Political Culture] (Moscow: Moscow Public Scientific Foundation, 2000), 229; L. Grigoryev, "Konflikty Interesov i Koalitsii" [Conflicts of Interests and Coalitions], Pro et Contra 38, nos. 4-5 (2007): 112.
46 Afanasyev, *Klientism I rossiiskaya*.

CHAPTER 3
RUSSIAN NATIONALISM IN A POST-IDEOLOGICAL ERA

STEPHEN E. HANSON

As the 15th anniversary of the collapse of the Soviet Union approached, there were numerous signs that Russian nationalism was making a comeback.[1] First, Russia's 2003 parliamentary elections produced a State Duma within which nationalism in one form or another appeared to possess a political monopoly. All four parties represented therein—the pro-Kremlin United Russia, the so-called Liberal Democratic Party of Russia (LDPR), led by the mercurial Vladimir Zhirinovskii, the Communist Party of the Russian Federation (CPRF), led by Gennadii Ziuganov, and Rodina (Motherland Party), led by Dmitrii Rogozin—called for the rebuilding of a powerful Russian state and for the restoration of Russia's former great-power role in international affairs. The leaders of the LDPR, CPRF, and Rodina had all actively and publicly proselytized for the revision of the current borders of the Russian Federation to include some or all of the former Soviet republics and the view that Russia must follow a non-Western "special path" of development; the leaders of United Russia tapped into xenophobic sentiments by accusing President Vladimir Putin's opponents of acting in the service of unnamed foreign governments.[2] Meanwhile, both of Russia's main liberal parties, Yabloko and the Union of Right Forces, failed to garner the 5-percent electoral minimum for representation in the State Duma—notwithstanding their own flirtations with nationalist personalities and themes.[3]

Second, reputable public-opinion polling agencies in Russia documented growing nationalist sentiment among the Russian population as well. Fully 89 percent of Russians surveyed, for example, wanted to see more emphasis on "patriotism" in the schools.[4] Of course, "patriotism" and "nationalism" are not necessarily synonyms. But disturbingly large proportions of the Russian populace also appeared willing to embrace an ethnic Russian (*russkii*) identity over the more inclusive "all-Russian" (*rossiiskii*) designation of Russian citizenship used in the Boris Yeltsin era.

When asked in fall 2005 whether they agreed with the slogan "Russia for the Russians" (*Rossiya dlya russkikh*), for example, well above half of those polled said yes.[5] Similarly, 30 percent of the Russian public expressed a willingness to ban people of Caucasian or Chinese heritage from the Russian Federation, while another 31 percent agreed that "the number of non-ethnic Russians living in Russian cities should be limited."[6]

Third, while President Putin himself continued ritually to condemn fascism and anti-Semitism in all their manifestations, Kremlin efforts to clamp down on opposition groupings and to restore the state's "power vertical" over Russian society nevertheless tended to increase the room for maneuver of nationalist organizations of various types. At a July 2005 summer training camp for the Kremlin-sponsored youth group Nashi (roughly translatable as "Our Guys"), young recruits listened attentively while deputy head of the Putin administration Vladimir Surkov declared the need to "protect youth from the impact of the West," while Putin aide Gleb Pavlovskii called Russia "the Jew of the 21st century," arguing that it served the West's need to find a scapegoat on which to blame global problems.[7] The first celebration of the new Kremlin holiday on November 4, the "Day of National Unity" commemorating the expulsion of the Poles from Moscow in 1612 by the popular heroes Minin and Pozharskii, and designed to replace the old celebration of the anniversary of the Bolshevik Revolution on November 7, saw even more extreme articulations of nationalist sentiment. At a march through downtown Moscow, approved in advance by municipal authorities, approximately a thousand people associated with shadowy groups like the Movement Against Illegal Immigration, the Eurasian Youth Union, and the Russian Public Movement gave fascist salutes and carried banners with slogans like "Ethnic Russians Advance!" (*Russkie Vpered*).[8]

How should we interpret such manifestations of both elite and popular xenophobia, and what might be their long-term effect on Russian foreign and domestic politics? Some analysts have seen Putin's efforts to encourage Russian public support for his state-building efforts in a generally positive light, pointing out that encouraging some degree of social patriotism is a necessary component of all successful political and economic reforms; these authors have tended to see extremist ethnic nationalism in Russia as relatively weak and marginal.[9] This sanguine interpretation of the influence of Russian nationalism during Putin's second term, however, fails to take into account the Kremlin's own evident concern that ideological nationalism might get out of control—as indicated in the decision to remove Rodina from the Moscow Duma election ballot in December 2005, after it aired an advertisement on Russian television that stereotyped people from the Caucasus by depicting Caucasians throwing watermelon rinds on the ground in a public park; the advertisement included a call for Moscow's streets to be cleared of "trash." Other authors have accused Westerners who emphasize the dangers of growing Russian nationalism of "Russophobia"—that is, a generalized objection to any form of Russian cultural self-assertion whatsoever.[10] But clearly, one can be entirely well disposed toward Russians and their country and still wish to engage in scholarly analysis of the likely future impact of extremist nationalism there.

A second group—directly opposed to the first—sees signs of growing Russian nationalism as confirmation of the view that "imperialism" remains deeply embedded in Russian culture and is likely to pose a serious threat to Russia's neighbors in the future.[11] Such scholars tend to portray Russian nationalism as unchangingly antiliberal and anti-Western, whether in the tsarist, Soviet, or post-Soviet periods.[12] Yet "pessimists" of this sort have a difficult time explaining the remarkable *weakness* of Russian nationalism for most of the 1990s. Indeed, some of the same analysts who now see Russian imperialism as innate were once so impressed by the country's initial willingness to dismantle the Soviet Union peacefully and to implement liberal reforms that they issued some of the most optimistic predictions about Russia's "transition" to democracy.[13] Today as well, essentialist views of Russian culture greatly oversimplify the complex dynamics of national identity formation in the post-Soviet context.

A third group of analysts, eschewing both the "optimistic" and "pessimistic" interpretations of Russian nationalism, have emphasized instead the largely pragmatic nature of both Kremlin policies and ordinary Russian day-to-day conduct in the post-Soviet era.[14] Indeed, opinion polls through Putin's second term as president continued to show an almost universal Russian loathing of avowed "fascists"; Russian support for extremist ideologies of all types remained no greater than, for example, in many developed European democracies, and only 11 percent of Russians surveyed even indicated agreement with the belief that fascism could ever come to power in their country.[15] Yet evidence of Russia's general deideologization since the collapse of communism cannot, by itself, disclose what the trends in Russian nationalism will be. Scholars who have quickly rejected the "Weimar scenario" for Russia, in which a revanchist dictatorship might come to power by capitalizing on bitterness generated by post-imperial collapse and economic dislocation, often forget that Weimar Germany looked like a success story as late as a decade after World War I, and that Nazism itself triumphed only after many years of marginalization after 1918. No historical parallel is ever exact, of course, but as we approach the 20th anniversary of the end of the USSR, the potential for similar results in Russia should, at a minimum, raise important questions for comparative research.[16]

In the present chapter, I therefore approach the problem of analyzing contemporary manifestations of Russian nationalism from a somewhat different perspective, one based upon the results of comparative research on nationalism carried out in other social contexts. Examining this literature allows us to see more clearly that while nationalist ideologues always profess to speak on behalf of "the people," nationalism itself is initially generated by intellectual elites. Only when nationalists take control of state institutions that promote the sustained, mass dissemination of their ideas does nationalism become a force within society at large. When nationalist state elites manage to link the cause of local nation building to "higher" universal ideological principles, however, even the most seemingly artificial constructions of national identity can ultimately inspire passionate conviction among ordinary people living in newly constructed "nation-states"—for good or for ill.

I then apply these theoretical findings to the Russian case. My central argument is twofold. First, on the ideological level, I find that Russian nationalism historically has been weak and divided as a result of unresolved tensions among the imperial, civic, and ethnic definitions of Russian identity proposed by various members of the Russian state elite and intelligentsia; nationalism's weakness has been exacerbated by the general collapse of ideology in the post-Soviet milieu, which has generated daunting conceptual difficulties facing intellectuals who now wish to reconstruct a coherent nationalist narrative of Russian history and a consensual vision of the "space" that Russia should occupy. Second, I argue that the very failure of every intellectual attempt since 1991 to weld Russian national identity to a compelling "universal" principle has generated a unique post-ideological political culture, in which loyalty to the Russian state and its struggle against supposed foreign enemies has become a substitute for formal ideological nationalism—a phenomenon that, building on Liah Greenfeld's analysis of "*ressentiment* nationalism" in 19th-century Central and East Europe, I term "*ressentiment* statism."[17] Putin's increasingly authoritarian state control over the means of mass communication has allowed *ressentiment* statism gradually to influence the attitudes of Russian society as well. The result of these trends, if left unchecked, will not be the victory of any coherent form of either liberalism or fascism, but instead an incoherent antiliberal backlash that could do serious damage to both Russia's and Eurasia's prospects for peace and prosperity in the 21st century.

WHAT IS NATIONALISM? SOME THEORETICAL REFLECTIONS

The literature on the origins and impact of nationalism in the modern era is far too vast to survey comprehensively here. It will be more useful to highlight a few key points of general agreement that have emerged from scholarly analysis of this topic over the past quarter-century, in order to apply these findings to the contemporary Russian case. Above all, three themes emerge as central. First, nationalism is socially constructed, and not a product of empirical cultural differences. Second, nationalist ideology is modern. Finally—and paradoxically—nationalism by itself tends to be a weak basis for state building; the strongest nationalisms are invariably those that are welded to other, more universalist ideologies. I will deal with these issues in turn.

Nationalism can be succinctly defined as an ideology that holds that the nation represents a higher form of community that deserves its own territorial state.[18] Defining the term "nation," however, is a rather more complicated task. Despite the concerted efforts of nationalists around the world over the past several centuries to find objective, empirical indicators that might actually demarcate the supposed boundaries of putative nations, almost all serious scholars now agree that national identity is in some basic sense "imagined": no genetic, linguistic, religious, or other cultural markers appear to be either necessary or sufficient for particular groups of people to think of themselves as "nations."[19] Even Anthony Smith's well-known argument that successful nationalism generally depends upon the prior existence of cultural "*ethnie*"—that is, communities united by shared "myth-symbol complexes" generating a common sense of history, territory, and culture—fails to account fully for such novel constructs as "American" or "Yugoslav" nationalism, which, despite their lack of connection with any pre-existing myth-symbol complex or indigenous culture, have nevertheless had dramatic effects in reordering the ethnic loyalties and identities of millions of people.[20] Moreover, while some sort of claim over specific territory is indeed a component of all nationalist ideologies, there is apparently no objective limit to the kinds of "spaces" that can be successfully envisioned as national homelands—ranging from regions where diaspora or enslaved populations have not lived for centuries (e.g., Palestine or Liberia), to vast archipelagoes with immense geographical, ethnic, and religious heterogeneity (e.g., Indonesia), to recently occupied territories suddenly redefined as sacred spaces for national rebirth (e.g., the western frontier for the United States or the Amur region for mid---19th-century Russia).[21] Indeed, the remarkable fact is that nationalist ideology can apparently transform almost any social characteristic into a "core" element of "nationness"—as is vividly demonstrated by the case of Stalin's construction of a potentially global "Soviet nation" (*Sovietskii narod*) around the principle of party-led proletarian revolutionary heroism.

In the end, then, while we can usefully define the distinctive ideological features of "nationalism," the term "nation" itself is best discarded as a social scientific category. In societies where nationalism gains broad appeal, passionate belief in the existence of the "nation" may also emerge among ordinary people, but this does not obligate researchers to adopt a nationalist social taxonomy themselves. However, in countries where nationalist ideology has successfully been disseminated to mass audiences, the term "national identity" may have theoretical utility, as a shorthand way of discussing the key symbols and beliefs that make up culturally dominant understandings of a given "nation"—as long as the ultimately constructed and contingent nature of such national identifications within society is always kept in mind.

Recognition of the underlying artificiality of national identity leads to a second key finding of the theoretical literature: nationalism is modern, dating back at most to the 16th century in a few West European countries, and becoming a global phenomenon only in the 19th and 20th centuries. Prior to the modern era, multiethnic polities with intermixed cultures and fuzzy external borders were everywhere the norm.

The invention of nationalism can be traced to two major changes in social life brought about by modernization. First, the rapid spread of the mechanical clock and the codification of a linear, abstract view of time in Europe tended to call into question appeals to "eternal" religious and philosophical principles as a basis for political legitimacy, thus forcing elites with specific ethnic loyalties to invent or imagine new myths of common origin to demonstrate the special historical status of their own communities.[22] Second, the rise of the modern state, with its twin claims of unique territorial jurisdiction and "sovereignty" in international law, gave political elites new incentives to standardize the identities of the populations they ruled in order to facilitate bureaucratic procedures, recruit new personnel, and break down local resistance to the expansion of markets.[23] Once the first European nation-states had been established—a development that dramatically increased their cultural legitimacy, regulatory efficiency, and military power—the invention of new "nations" quickly accelerated, as other states (or would-be state builders) were forced to follow suit in order to compete effectively.[24] By the end of the 20th century, the nation-state had become the hegemonic form of political order around the globe, despite its rather poor fit with pre-existing informal cultural identities outside a handful of highly developed countries.

That nationalism is both "constructed" and modern helps to account for the intensity of national conflicts in territories where stable nation-states have not yet been established. As Rogers Brubaker has demonstrated, the ideology that each "nation" deserves its own sovereign territorial state, when applied to regions previously ruled by multinational empires with fluid cultural boundaries, automatically generates zero-sum struggles involving three central players: "nationalizing nationalist" elites who attempt to enforce and institutionalize their proposed new national identity within the territory they control, external "national homelands" that actively resist these efforts by posing as the "protectors" of ethnic kin living outside "their" nation-state, and newly designated "national minorities" that are caught between these two competitors. This "triadic nexus" is an explosive mixture that, at its worst, can degenerate into intense armed conflict, as occurred in Central Europe in the interwar period and in again in post-communist Yugoslavia. The creation of "nation-states" in the territory of the former Soviet Union has generated many parallel political and social tensions.[25]

Yet as Brubaker recognizes, not all articulations of nationalism are equally powerful or socially persuasive. This brings us to a third finding that emerges from a review of recent studies of nationalism, one that has been perhaps less widely disseminated than the first two: namely, that nationalist ideology is paradoxically at its strongest when it appeals to universal principles, and not only to local loyalties.[26] Indeed, the call to defend "the nation" by itself has proven to be a relatively weak basis for social mobilization; successful nationalists instead generally argue for fidelity to the nation as a strategy for preserving cherished universal human values. Thus, liberal nationalists in the United States see the American nation as a unique carrier of freedom and democracy, republican nationalists in France see their nation as a bearer of universal conceptions of community and citizenship, and fascist nationalists in Mussolini's Italy and Hitler's Germany saw the nation as a vehicle for the preservation of imperial or racial "greatness." Where nationalists do not manage to weld together local and universal values in constructing the national myth—as has been true in most postcolonial African countries, for example—ordinary people tend to treat the nation-state that formally rules them purely instrumentally, or with indifference.[27]

The insight that successful national ideologies generally base their claims to political status on "higher" ideological principles lies behind Liah Greenfeld's extremely important study of nationalism in Europe since the 17th century.[28] Greenfeld demonstrates that only the first successful modern nationalisms—those of England and the United States—could be fully "liberal universalist," precisely because they did not yet have any other "national" competitors. The call to establish "popular rule" in these two countries could be presented as the sole alternative to the continued rule of unelected monarchs, at home and abroad—and thus English and American liberals could quite unproblematically mix national patriotism with democratic aspirations to universal rights. Matters had already become more complex by the time of the French Revolution, whose leaders had to deal with the hostility of the English "nation" to their own efforts to realize the "rights of man." To claim superior status to the English, the French revolutionaries had to assert not only that they were establishing the rule of the people by overthrowing the Crown, as the British and Americans had done, but also that British institutions of government were at best only partial realizations of the universal values of liberty, equality, and fraternity that would be established in France in their pure form. Ideological competition with British liberalism, Greenfeld argues, generated a French national identity after 1789 that mixed its universal liberal principles with an emphasis on the supposedly unique, higher French sense of civic community—with problematic long-term consequences for French political stability.

By the 19th century, emerging nationalist movements found the ideological terrain of liberal and republican universalism wholly occupied by the powerful, expanding American, British, and French empires. Thus, for German nationalists, combining universalist liberalism and domestic patriotism became much more difficult: adopting a "liberal" or "civic" politics built on individualism and a defense of constitutional proceduralism appeared tantamount to surrendering one's own national identity to embrace the rule of alien Western principles. Instead, Romantic German nationalists argued that true loyalty to one's nation demanded a rejection of liberalism in favor of an assertion of more "authentic" values of tradition and spirituality, seen as rooted in the "uncorrupted" habits and folk traditions of indigenous ethnic communities. Such a conception of national rebirth profoundly influenced nationalist ideologues throughout Central and East Europe.[29] In this way, "latecomers" to nationalism tended to express their political philosophies in ethnic rather than civic forms.

Moreover, East European ethnic nationalism was strongly colored—to return to Liah Greenfeld's terminology—by *ressentiment*: the feeling of deep animosity and rage toward liberal nations claiming superior status on the basis of supposedly "universal civic values" that seemed merely to conceal a selfish defense of their own growing wealth and military power. Indeed, Romantic nationalists now claimed that promoting the rebirth of authentic folk traditions in Central and East Europe was the only way to prevent the global dominance of "Anglo-Saxon" materialism and individualism. Support for the territorial claims of one's own ethnic group, then, was portrayed as integral to the defense of cultural pluralism and traditional values throughout the civilized world. In this way, local ethnic nationalism could gain its own distinctive sort of universal legitimacy.

Greenfeld's central argument about the importance of ideological universalism in the articulation of nationalist ideology, and the ways in which nationalism is therefore affected by the global ideological environment, is a seminal contribution to our general theoretical understanding of nationalist movements. However, Greenfeld's analysis suffers from a tendency to assume that national identities, once originally articulated and disseminated within a given society, can never be transformed—except perhaps through sustained foreign occupation, as in the case of West Germany after 1945. As a result, her analysis of the development of Nazism and Leninism, which she sees as simple extensions of earlier German and Russian *ressentiment* nationalism, is unpersuasive. Oddly enough, despite her own emphasis on the mutability of nationalism as it is expressed in various historical and cultural settings, she fails to take seriously enough the ideological distinctiveness of 20th century fascism and communism, which both went far beyond the original 19th-century Romantic nationalist rejection of civic liberalism to propose entirely new forms of political identity that would reconstruct the "nation" in radically new ways. As I show below, taking seriously the differences among competing nationalist ideologies is vital to a complete understanding of nationalism's course in the Soviet and post-Soviet periods.

DILEMMAS OF RUSSIAN NATIONALISM UNDER TSARISM AND COMMUNISM

The collective findings of the literature on nationalism, when applied to Russian history, lead to one central conclusion: to date, the Russian state has never been dominated by ideological nationalists, and, largely for this reason, there is still no social consensus on how to define the Russian "nation." Neither the tsarist nor Soviet elites ever managed to standardize mainstream expressions of cultural identity in the territories they ruled according to a single dominant "national" principle; only during periods of crisis were they even interested in doing so.[30] Indeed, the close historical association of Russian state power with multinational empire has tended to make Russian "patriots" worry—with substantial justification—that upholding Russian (*russkii*) ethnicity as the basis for state legitimacy would ultimately undermine, rather than bolster, Russia's great-power status. At the same time, Russian liberals have struggled to articulate a "civic" basis for Russian national identity that might be clearly distinguished from imperial understandings of how to construct a multiethnic society. As I will show, these dilemmas continue to ensnare liberal and ethnic nationalists alike in the post-Soviet period.

The tsarist regime, as has been emphasized by countless historians, was for most of its history explicitly multinational—"all-Russian" (*vserossiiskii*) rather than ethnically "Russian" (*russkii*)—with a monarchy that until the 19th century was deeply intertwined with other European royal houses and a nobility that generally spoke French rather than Russian. Non-Russian ethnic communities conquered by the expanding Russian Empire, too, were generally granted a fair degree of cultural autonomy, except where they posed a direct military challenge to tsarist authority, as in the Caucasus.[31] In all these ways, again, the Russian Empire before the 19th century simply reproduced the typical pattern of traditional empires in the pre-industrial period. The spread of Enlightenment ideas and, in particular, the encounter with Napoleonic France began to change this pattern—as is demonstrated by the tsarist education minister Sergey Uvarov's famous attempt to redefine the basis for the legitimacy of the Russian Empire in terms of "autocracy, orthodoxy, and nationality (*narodnost'*)." At this stage, however, the meaning of the third term in this triad was still vague at best, with the emphasis still squarely on autocracy; certainly *narodnost'* did not imply any exclusive focus on Russian ethnicity as the sole basis for political loyalty.[32] By the mid-1800s, the influence of German Romanticism and the rise of West European nation-states had generated modern state-seeking nationalism among many of the ethnic minorities of the Russian Empire; one could also clearly see a new emphasis on official ethnicity in the regime's own heavy-handed efforts to "Russify" its subjects in response. Expressions of *ressentiment* against Western liberalism, too, began to emerge in the more reactionary writings of the Slavophiles.[33] Yet, as Astrid Tuminez has shown, official imperial ideology continued to assert the multinational nature of tsarism's legitimacy, and ethnic nationalists promoting a pan-Slavic definition of Russia's national identity only gained influence over tsarist foreign policy in periods immediately following Russian military defeat: from 1856 to 1878, after the Crimean War, and again from 1905 to 1914, after the Russo-Japanese War.[34] In sum, Russian ethnic nationalism was a product of the breakdown of tsarist imperialism—not the cause of its initial expansion.

Nor did Russian nationalism, in any direct sense, constitute the basis of legitimacy for the multinational Soviet Union. Despite the all-too-frequent colloquial use of the terms "USSR" and "Russia" as synonyms, recent scholarship has demonstrated the critical importance of Marxist-Leninist "internationalism" to both the theory and practice of nationalities policy in the Soviet period.[35] Not only was the early Bolshevik party itself remarkably diverse in its ethnic composition, including Russians, Latvians, Poles, Georgians, and Jews in prominent leadership positions, but the Bolsheviks also took very seriously their guiding objective of building communism on an international scale.

The key to understanding the Bolshevik interpretation of the historical role of "nations," as in so many other areas of Marxist-Leninist ideology, is to take into account explicitly the time factor involved in achieving communism's final victory.[36] For Lenin and Stalin—as for all Marxists—national identity must be seen as an expression of partial, class-bound consciousness; thus nationalism would eventually disappear along with classes themselves. As Lenin explicitly recognized, however, proletarian internationalism could not be achieved all at once, everywhere on the globe; thus, even after socialism's revolutionary victory in the Soviet state, nationalities would continue to exist.[37] Indeed, one could, in a sense, "rank" different nations according to the stages of historical class consciousness they expressed. Thus, ethnicities mired in the stage of "primitive communism," such as indigenous reindeer-herding peoples of the Arctic, were considered to be at the lowest level of historical development. Next in the hierarchy were nations still dependent on slavery, or the "Asiatic mode of production," which were surpassed in turn by "bourgeois" nations of the sort typical of capitalist Europe and North America. Socialist nations with enough revolutionary consciousness to establish the "dictatorship of the proletariat" were at the highest level of historical development, on their way to a full "merging" (*sliianie*) of nationalities under communism. And Russia, which had carried out the Great October Revolution, was thereby the leading nation in the world.[38]

Yet while the trumpeting of Russia's leading role among "socialist nations" clearly did reflect nationalist sentiments among a crucial sector of Russian supporters of the Communist Party of the Soviet Union, Russian nationalism was no more the basis for CPSU legitimacy than it had been the ideological foundation of tsarism. Indeed, Lenin's desire to recognize the possibility of other "socialist nationalisms" in the expanding Soviet state, institutionalized in the creation of "soviet socialist republics" with formally equal status to the Russian Soviet Federative Socialist Republic (RSFSR), generated deep tensions between "Soviet" and "Russian" definitions of national identity that persisted throughout the Soviet period.[39] As under tsarism, only in times of deep crisis—as, for example, after the Nazi invasion of the USSR, or after the disastrous Soviet invasion of Afghanistan—did Russian ethnic nationalist themes begin to surface in official or semiofficial elite discourse. Ironically, the rise of an anti-Leninist Russian nationalist critique of Soviet internationalism in the Brezhnev and Gorbachev eras—one that claimed Russia to be the "most exploited" of all Soviet nations, castigated Marxist-Leninist "internationalism" for sacrificing Russian youth in foreign adventures, and decried the despoiling of the Russian environment and damming of Siberian rivers—only hastened the final collapse of the Soviet version of a Russia-centered imperium, leading Russia to call for "sovereignty" along with the other fourteen Soviet republics.[40] By 1990, Mikhail Gorbachev's perestroika had weakened CPSU authority so greatly that a fundamental reordering of relations between Russia and the non-Russian nations of the USSR was inevitable. But the problem of defining the identity and historical purpose of the Russian "nation" remained unresolved.

RUSSIAN NATIONALISM IN THE POST-SOVIET CONTEXT

That post-Soviet "Russia" would require a new, consensual ideological definition was well understood by ambitious politicians throughout the RSFSR in the late Gorbachev period. It was equally well understood that those who proposed a successful new vision of the Russian nation would naturally emerge as Russia's legitimate new leadership. The final death throes of Marxism-Leninism under Gorbachev therefore generated a remarkable range of proposals for rethinking the criteria defining Russian citizenship, national boundaries, and foreign policy. At the same time, however, post-Soviet Russian nationalists faced a novel cultural obstacle: namely, a ubiquitous loathing of "ideology" in any form throughout the post-Soviet social milieu. As a result, nationalists of all stripes were forced to undercut their stated ideological principles with assurances that they were, after all, really "centrists" and "pragmatists"—or perhaps not even entirely serious about their professed political positions. Such a stance made it impossible to connect pride in Russian national identity to any universal principles for which it might be worth sacrificing one's short-term instrumental interests. Post-ideological ironic distance thus tended to undermine all four of the major variants of Russian nationalism to emerge from the wreckage of "Soviet internationalism": the neo-Slavophilism of Aleksandr Solzhenitsyn, the "Soviet traditionalism" of Gennadii Ziuganov, the "superimperialism" of Vladimir Zhirinovskii, and the "*rossiiskii* civic liberalism" formally embraced by Russian President Boris Yeltsin.

Solzhenitsyn's famous treatise on rebuilding Russia, first published in 1990, proposed to define "Russianness" essentially in terms of fidelity to the spiritual traditions of the Orthodox Church and preservation of the supposedly higher sense of community typical of Slavic cultures.[41] Russia's rebirth, Solzhenitsyn insisted, could only begin when "foreign" models of social development, including both Marxism and Western liberalism, had been cast aside as inappropriate to Russian culture. Promoting Russian national revival, he insisted, would help to preserve higher spiritual traditions in a world dominated by mindless Western materialism. Thus, Solzhenitsyn's nationalism paralleled in many respects the typical forms of 19th-century ethnic nationalism in Central and East Europe discussed earlier in the present chapter.

Taken literally, though, such a definition of the Russian "nation" would necessarily encompass all Slavic and Orthodox territories of the former Soviet Union—explicitly including Belarus, Ukraine, and northern Kazakhstan, and implicitly perhaps even the Slavic and Orthodox countries of Southeast Europe. To be sure, Solzhenitsyn pointedly insisted that the Russian "nation" had only been weakened by its entanglement with imperialism, and he called for the immediate independence of non-Slavic Soviet peoples in Central Asia, the Caucasus, and the Baltic region. But Solzhenitsyn's insistence on the organic unity of the remaining territories of "Russia" nevertheless had unmistakably imperial connotations—which he found himself forced to deny, rather unconvincingly, by emphasizing his commitment to the "voluntary" reintegration of Slavic territories. Moreover, in a world of ubiquitous corruption and short-term expediency, Solzhenitsyn's appeals to "eternal" spiritual values of ancient Russia, coming from a man who had spent the past two decades in exile in the United States, tended to strike ordinary Russians as hopelessly anachronistic and even absurd.

Much more compelling—especially for the millions of older Russian citizens who had embraced the "Soviet nation" as their own in the wake of Stalin's victory over the Nazis in World War II—was Gennadii Ziuganov's proposal to redefine "Russia" as, in effect, the Soviet Union itself.[42] Ziuganov did so by making a conceptual distinction between the early, misguided "internationalism" of the initial phase of Bolshevik rule and the later organic melding of "Russian" and "Soviet" traditions under Stalin. Building on the arguments of the Eurasianists of the 1920s, Ziuganov argued that the historic mission of the Russian nation was to build a "great power" (*derzhava*) that might counter the hegemonic, materialist aspirations of Western commercial liberal powers such as Great Britain and the United States. In particular, Stalin's reconciliation with the Orthodox Church in the fight against the Nazi invaders was seen as the natural outcome of the Soviet elite's healthy state-building efforts. After Soviet victory in World War II, Ziuganov insisted, the unity of "Soviet" and "Russian" identity meant that pride in communism as a universal principle would naturally reinforce pride in one's nation. Gorbachev and Yeltsin's betrayal of the communist cause, then, could only be ascribed to the machinations of a powerful anti-Soviet (and therefore anti-Russian) conspiracy led by foreign intelligence circles and "cosmopolitan" (i.e., Jewish) elites.

But while this effort to unite "Soviet" and "Russian" nationalism did serve to mobilize the most successful mass party in post-Soviet Russia, it was ultimately undercut by Ziuganov's inability to articulate a convincing defense of the continuing validity of communism as a universal ideological principle. Shorn of its Marxist-Leninist philosophical underpinnings, Ziuganov's communism was transformed into a parochial doctrine without any potential international appeal. Moreover, like Solzhenitsyn, Ziuganov took pains to emphasize his aversion to violence and extremism, as well as his desire to restore the "Soviet system" through legal and gradual means—and thus contradicted the essentially revolutionary logic of his argument to rebuild the USSR as the last bulwark against impending liberal capitalist hegemony. Over time, this odd mixture of revolutionary extremism and practical acquiescence to the status quo would disillusion a growing number of Ziuganov's original nationalist supporters.

A third conceptual option for would-be post-Soviet rebuilders of the Russian "national idea" was to adopt a fascist model of ideological "universalism"—that is, the idea that restoration of the lost empire would lead to the establishment of a "new world order" in which traditional principles of hierarchy, loyalty, and morality would be re-established on a global scale. Yet in this case, too, the general collapse of ideological convictions in the wake of the Soviet Union's breakup, along with the specific cultural animosity toward self-professed "*fashisty*" among most Russians as a result of the Nazi invasion, made constructing this sort of national myth very difficult. The most immediately relevant historical model for imperial rebirth, in fact, was the USSR itself, but rebuilding the Soviet Union was a cause that had already been appropriated by Ziuganov and his colleagues. Nor did the idea of resurrecting the tsarist empire have any serious appeal to a highly educated, urbanized Russian population. A handful of self-described Russian "national socialists," such as Aleksandr Barkashov, directly appropriated Nazi style ideological principles and styles—while claiming that the swastika was historically a Russian symbol—but such self-appointed führers remained politically and socially marginal.

The most successful strategy for Russian fascism was thus to adopt it in a tongue-in-cheek version. Hence the remarkable rise and enduring popularity of Vladimir Zhirinovskii, whose ideological stance has been widely misinterpreted both in Russia and the West. Some commentators argue that behind the LDPR leader's buffoonery is a sincere and dangerous fascist threat; others retort that behind Zhirinovskii's fascist rhetoric is simple buffoonery. Both sides miss Zhirinovskii's remarkable innovation—namely, to articulate a "joke fascism" that transcends the normal distinction between parody of and commitment to antiliberal values.[43] Anyone who reads Zhirinovskii's main political tracts will soon discover all the typical fascist ideological themes: deep-seated xenophobia; a call for centralized, personal authority to counteract social disorder; complex conspiracy theories to "explain" Russia's catastrophic loss of global status; and a grand strategy for geopolitical expansion.[44] But Zhirinovskii is careful always to leaven his fascism with humor. His call to bring the Baltic States to their knees by placing giant fans on their borders to blow radioactive waste toward them, for example, is simultaneously a terrifying expression of the desire for geopolitical revenge and an ironic, silly commentary on the chaotic state of Russia's poorly guarded nuclear weapons facilities. Zhirinovskii's openly sexual rhetoric, too, constitutes both an expression of machismo and a call to have a good time in a world where "anything goes." In this sense, his reliable cooperation with both the Yeltsin and Putin administrations, despite his radical rhetoric, also has a double meaning: it earns him money to support his political network, and simultaneously demonstrates the farcical nature of post-Soviet "democracy." Zhirinovskii's joke fascism has had remarkable long-term success in post-Soviet Russian politics. As late as November 2005, he remained the second most trusted politician in the country (albeit in a country where no politician other than Putin was widely trusted).[45] Educated Russians who might otherwise turn away in disgust from Zhirinovskii's xenophobic utterances continue to be attracted to his "wit" (*ostroumie*) and "originality" (*original'nost*).[46] Despite the enduring popularity in Russia of his ideological stance, however, there is still no way for ironic fascism to appeal to universal principles in the way the original fascism and Nazism of the 20th century once did. Thus, his party, the LDPR, remains in essence a protest party, rather than a vehicle for promoting and institutionalizing any powerful new definition of the Russian nation.

Given that pan-Slavism, communism, and fascism have all been undermined by or intermixed with the post-ideological cultural cynicism of post-Soviet Russia, one might have expected the fourth proposed definition of the Russian nation—a liberal vision of *rossiiskii* citizenship within legally defined international boundaries of the Russian Federation—to have triumphed. Indeed, in many ways, Russia in 1991 was closer to constituting a nation-state than at any previous time in its history: more than four-fifths of its population was ethnically Russian, support for imperial revanchism within the exhausted post-Soviet society was extremely limited, and Russia's newly elected president, Boris Yeltsin, proudly proclaimed his allegiance to "European" values of democracy and liberty.

Yet over the course of the 1990s, liberal Russian nationalism also proved incapable of welding domestic patriotism to universal ideological principles, for several reasons. First, Yeltsin and his advisers made the strategic error of tying support for liberal nationalism directly to the fate of radical market reforms. When "shock therapy" quickly ran aground and the Russian economy went into a long and bitter tailspin, social support for Russian liberalism naturally declined along with it. Second, the image of "the West" as a bulwark of liberal values that would welcome a new democratic Russia as an equal was fatally undermined by unstinting U.S. support for Yeltsin's neoliberal economic policies, a perception of Western indifference to Russian viewpoints and interests in foreign policy, and the decisions to expand the North Atlantic Treaty Organization (NATO) and the European Union to include nearly every post-communist European state except Russia. Third, bitter divisions among Russian liberals themselves—in part a result of differing evaluations of the economic and foreign policy problems mentioned above—ruined liberalism's image among ordinary Russian citizens. Indeed, Yeltsin's decision to launch a contest to find a new Russian "national idea" at the beginning of his second term symbolized the bankruptcy of his original articulation of liberal nationalism. By the end of the first post-Soviet decade, nearly every key concept associated with liberal ideology—"democracy," "market economy," even "liberalism" itself—had been thoroughly discredited.

Russia during the Yeltsin era thus experienced the systematic delegitimation of every major ideology of the 20th century. In fact, Russia's polity, economy, and society were in many ways the most complete realization of the world depicted by modern "rational choice theory," in which every individual actor calculates every move from an instrumental, strategic point of view.[47] It is hardly surprising, then, that by 1999 few Russians were at all interested in arcane debates about Russian national identity. Yet the problem of defining that identity did not disappear simply because of Russian popular revulsion against ideological efforts to resolve it.

PUTIN'S STATISM AND THE FUTURE OF RUSSIAN NATIONALISM

It is only by taking into account the entire history of Russian nationalism summarized above that one can successfully analyze the political views of President Vladimir Putin concerning the vexed question, "What is Russia?" Even more than a decade after his rise to power in fall 1999, analysts still debate his basic political orientation. Yet all now agree on one thing: Putin sees as his primary mission the rebuilding of the Russian state. Indeed, Putin's call to reinforce the state's "power vertical" (i.e., the hierarchical chain of command) and his evocation of a new spirit of "loyalty to the state" (*gosudarstvennost'*) as the key to Russia's revival have been the most consistent themes of both his rhetoric and his policy.

What remains contentious is, precisely, the long-term political goal for which Putin wishes to reconstruct the state. Some analysts insist that Putin is really a liberal, but one who recognizes that without a strong state administration, Russian democracy and markets are doomed to corruption and decay.[48] Others see Putin as having a "grand strategy" to use the state for the restoration of authoritarian rule—perhaps ultimately along neo-Soviet lines.[49] Yet Putin never explicitly embraces any of the definitions of the

Russian nation proffered by the leading ideological figures of the Yeltsin era. Like Russian liberals, he generally uses *"rossiiskii"* rather than *"russkii"* when referring to the Russian citizenry—although the latter term has admittedly become more prominent in his more recent speeches—and he proclaims the need to embrace the principles of modern global civilization. However, he clearly rejects the notion that defending individual rights and freedoms will somehow lead to peace and prosperity by uniting Russia with the West. Like Russian communists, he frequently declares his respect for the achievements of Soviet power, but he equally firmly rejects the idea of resurrecting the Soviet Union itself. Like Russian neo-Slavophiles, he expresses firm support for Orthodoxy as a guiding source of values, and he even approved the ostentatious reburial of White Army General Anton Denikin—yet his own religious commitments remain vague at best, and his efforts at reconciliation with the communist past separate him fundamentally from figures like Solzhenitsyn. Finally, like Russian fascists, he proclaims the need for firm centralized authority if Russia is to reclaim its great-power status, yet he and his advisers have made the "struggle against fascism and extremism" a central political theme in mobilizing Russia's youth.

In short, Putin's statism remains fundamentally post-ideological—very much in line with the sentiments of the vast majority of post-Soviet Russian citizens. The pastiche of contradictory holidays, ceremonies, and symbols that has been introduced by Putin and his advisers is designed to satisfy Russia's multiple subcultures, not to provide any consistent new definition of the Russian nation. In fact, Putin's defense of the state, unlike that of his tsarist, Soviet, or liberal predecessors, is not designed as a means to some future ideological goal—rather, Putin sees *gosudarstvennost'* as a goal in and of itself. Indeed, loyalty to the state, in the form of obedience to central authority, seems to serve as the key indicator by which Putin divides "patriots" from "traitors." This explains why those who attack any aspect of Kremlin official policy—particularly on subjects Putin sees as vital to his efforts to rebuild state power, such as the war in Chechnya or the anti-oligarch campaign—are so frequently painted by Putin's entourage as somehow less than fully "Russian."[50] The formation of the Nashi youth group was the culmination of this trend: only those who stand up for Kremlin policy could be considered "ours"; all others are alien (*chuzhie*).

Putin's *gosudarstvennost'* also contains a pronounced element of *ressentiment*, in Greenfeld's sense. Russian state building for Putin is not simply a pragmatic response to past policy failure—it is a moral crusade designed to right the historical injustices perpetrated against the Russian people by supposedly "democratic" and "advanced" powers, in league with their hidden supporters within Russian society. Those who criticize Russian policy according to so-called universal moral values of human rights are seen as hypocrites with nefarious motives who are applying "double standards" that Western nations also fail to meet.[51] And at times, Putin and his circle even appear to embrace antiliberal conspiracy theories as explanations for Russia's global isolation—as, for instance, in Putin's address to the nation following the Beslan school seizure in September 2004: "We showed weakness and the weak are trampled upon. Some want to cut off a juicy morsel from us while others are helping them. They are helping because they believe that, as one of the world's major nuclear powers, Russia is still posing a threat to someone, and therefore this threat must be removed. And terrorism is, of course, only a tool for achieving these goals."[52] Putin's "*ressentiment* statism" thus shares the reactionary orientation of previous expressions of *ressentiment* nationalism in European history—but without any particular emphasis on the Russian nation itself.

What does this imply about the future of Russian nationalism in Russian state–society relations in the Putin era and beyond? Throughout the present chapter, I have focused on elite efforts to articulate and enforce conceptions of national identity and the intersection of such efforts with state institutions and policies. Broader groups within society, I have argued, tend to mobilize around nationalist ideals only when these ideals are clearly and consistently articulated by elites with control over important state institutions, and when these ideals are welded conceptually to "higher" universal ideological principles. In Russian history, such national mobilization has occurred rarely, in periods of crisis and war; indeed, moments of national crisis such as the Time of Troubles and the Great Fatherland War remain the key symbolic reference points for contemporary efforts to construct Russian national identity. Official state ideology, however, has remained fundamentally at odds with Russian nationalism throughout the tsarist and Soviet periods. The Yeltsin era did witness the articulation by state elites of something like a coherent liberal Russian (*rossiiskii*) nationalism, but the extended political and economic crisis of the 1990s fatally undermined its social impact. By the turn of the 21st century, tsarist, communist, fascist, and liberal ideologies alike were associated in Russian society with geopolitical failure and low international prestige. The result was a uniquely de-ideologized and cynical cultural milieu in which the impact of "principled" nationalism, of any sort, was necessarily limited. At the same time, however, growing anger at Russia's perceived humiliation and marginalization in a world of triumphant liberal capitalist "globalization" was also widespread among a variety of social groups. Putin's *ressentiment* statism thus expresses not only the informal political culture of the post-Soviet elite, but also taps into a powerful cultural current in contemporary Russian society—and this helps to explain Putin's genuine popularity well beyond his second term and into his tenure as prime minister to his hand-picked successor as president, Dmitriy Medvedev.

At the same time, the effort to cope with the absence of a Russian national idea by adopting what Igor Chubais has called the "mixed salad alternative" (*put' vinagreta*)—mixing and matching tsarist, communist, statist, and liberal symbols willy-nilly—only postpones the problem of defining the Russian nation in a clear and consistent manner; it cannot solve it.[53] Like all modern governments without any clear underlying ideology that can make a plausible claim to universal validity, Putin's regime is likely to remain administratively ineffective, prone to corruption, and unable to chart a consistent strategic direction in foreign policy. Structural forces propelling Russia's strong economic rebound in the first decade of the 21st century—in particular, soaring global energy prices—may have worked to conceal Russia's continuing administrative weakness in the short to medium run, but sooner or later, serious challenges to Putin's hierarchical, centralized model of the Russian state are bound to arise. His failure to articulate a workable strategy for building not just the state, but also a coherent definition of the Russian "nation" it governs, leaves an ideological vacuum concerning Russian national identity that is likely to be exploited by nationalists of various types in the years to come. In particular—as the right-wing efflorescence of November 4, 2005, vividly demonstrated—there is a danger that Putin's mélange of national holidays, images, and movements will be infused with more consistently ideological antiliberal meanings by ethnic Russian nationalists who are committed to the most xenophobic elements of Putin's *gosudarstvennost'*.

NOTES

1   An abridged version of this paper may also be found in the following volume: "Russian Nationalism in a Post-Ideological Era," in Eugene B. Rumer and Celeste A. Wallander, *Russia Watch: Essays in Honor of George Kolt* (Washington, DC: Center for Strategic and International Studies Press, 2007), 10–25. The author would like to thank Mikhail Ilyin, Beth Mitchneck, and Elizabeth Wood for their helpful comments on an earlier version of this chapter.

2   For example, when independent liberal State Duma Deputy Vladimir Ryzhkov declared his opposition to the proposed new regulations on non-governmental organizations (NGOs) in fall 2005, Deputy Speaker Liubov Sliska of United Russia pointedly asked him what country's passport he held (as reported in the *International Herald Tribune*, December 24, 2005).

3   Thus, for example, Yabloko announced its willingness to cooperate with the extremist National Bolshevik Party of Eduard Limonov in an anti-Putin alliance, while Union of Right Forces leader Anatolii Chubais declared the goal of building a new "liberal empire" in the former Soviet Union.

4   E. Vovk, "A Patriotic Upbringing: Words or Deeds?" Public Opinion Foundation Database, May 2, 2004, accessed at http://bd.english.fom.ru/report/cat/man/patriotizm/ed040530.

5   A. Golov, "Massovoe Vospriatie National'nykh Men'shinstv: Peremeny Za God" [Mass Perception of National Minorities: Changes Over the Year], Levada Analytical Center, December 12, 2005, accessed at http://www.levada.ru/press/2005121400.print.html.

6   "Racist Sentiments Grow in Russia—Survey," Mosnews.com, August 15, 2005, accessed at http://www.mosnews.com/news/2005/08/15/sentiments.shtml.

7   Surkov quoted in Igor Torbakov, "Rebirth of Agitprop: Spending on Patriotic Propaganda Will Triple," *Eurasia Daily Monitor* 2, no. 142 (July 22, 2005), accessed at http://www.jamestown.org/publications_details.php?volume_id=407&issue_id=3411&article_id=2370052; Pavlovskii quoted in *The Moscow Times*, "3,000 Nashi Commissars Go to Camp," July 18, 2005, accessed at http://www.moscowtimes.ru/stories/2005/07/18/002.html.

8   See article and photos, "Ultranationalist March in Downtown Moscow," Mosnews.com, November 6, 2005, accessed at http://www.mosnews.com/images/g/s116.shtml.

9   See, for example, Richard Sakwa, *Putin: Russia's Choice* (London and New York: Routledge, 2004).

10   See, for example, several commentaries by scholars cited in Peter Lavelle, "Deconstructing 'Russophobia' and 'Russocentric,'" Intelligent.ru, accessed at http://english.intelligent.ru/articles/russia_world.htm.

11   Stephen Blank, "Is Russia a Democracy and Does It Matter?" *World Affairs* 167, no. 3 (2005): 125–136.

12   Richard Pipes, "Flight from Freedom: What Russians Think and Want," *Foreign Affairs* 83, no. 9 (2004): 9–15.

13   See, for example, Richard Pipes, "The Last Gasp of Russia's Communists," *New York Times*, October 5, 1993.

14   Andrei Tsygankov, "Vladimir Putin's Vision of Russia as a Normal Great Power," *Post-Soviet Affairs* 21, no. 2 (2005): 132–56.

15   "Russian People Afraid of Poverty and Low-Quality Life Most," Pravda.ru, May

17, 2005, accessed at http://english.pravda.ru/main/18/90/363/15481_Russians.html.

16 For an earlier attempt to engage in such a comparative approach, see Stephen E. Hanson and Jeffrey S. Kopstein, "The Weimar/Russia Comparison," *Post-Soviet Affairs* 13, no. 3 (1997): 252–83; Stephen Shenfield, "The Weimar/Russia Comparison: Reflections on Hanson and Kopstein," and Jeffrey S. Kopstein and Stephen E. Hanson, "Paths to Uncivil Societies and Anti-Liberal States: A Response to Shenfield," *Post-Soviet Affairs* 14, no. 4 (1998): 355–75. My most recent findings are presented in Stephen E. Hanson, *Post-Imperial Democracies: Ideology and Party Formation in Third Republic France, Weimar Germany, and Post-Soviet Russia* (Cambridge: Cambridge University Press, 2010).

17 Liah Greenfeld, *Nationalism: Five Roads to Modernity* (Cambridge, MA: Harvard University Press, 1992).

18 For closely related definitions, see John Breuilly, *Nationalism and the State* (Manchester Manchester University Press, 1982), and Ernest Haas, *Nationalism, Liberalism, and Progress* (Ithaca, NY: Cornell University Press, 1997).

19 Benedict Anderson, *Imagined Communities: Reflections on the Origin and Spread of Nationalism* (London and New York: Verso, 1983).

20 Anthony D. Smith, *The Ethnic Origins of Nations* (Oxford and Cambridge, MA: Blackwell, 1986).

21 On the importance to nationalist ideology of claims to a territorial "homeland," see Robert J. Kaiser, *The Geography of Nationalism in Russia and the USSR* (Princeton, NJ: Princeton University Press, 1994). On the specific example of Russian nationalist "imaginings" of the Amur region, see Mark Bassin, *Imperial Visions: Nationalist Imagination and Russian Imperial Expansion in the Russian Far East, 1840–1865* (Cambridge and New York: Cambridge University Press, 1999). Both Kaiser and Bassin insist that geographical and sociological realities do place some limits on the kinds of nationalist imaginings that can successfully take hold in particular regions. A general comparative survey of successful nationalist territorial claims, however, makes it very difficult indeed to specify what these objective limits are in any general sense.

22 Anderson, *Imagined Communities*, 192–99.

23 Ernest Gellner, *Nations and Nationalism* (Ithaca, NY: Cornell University Press, 1982); Hedrik Spruyt, *The Sovereign State and Its Competitors: An Analysis of System Change* (Princeton, NJ: Princeton University Press, 1994).

24 Spruyt, *The Sovereign State and Its Competitors*.

25 Rogers Brubaker, *Nationalism Reframed: Nationhood and the National Question in the New Europe* (Cambridge and New York: Cambridge University Press, 1996).

26 I owe this particular formulation of the point to Ken Jowitt.

27 Joel Migdal, *Strong Societies and Weak States: State–Society Relations and State Capabilities in the Third World* (Princeton, NJ: Princeton University Press, 1988).

28 Liah Greenfeld, *Nationalism: Five Roads to Modernity* (Cambridge, MA: Harvard University Press, 1992).

29 See also Miroslav Hroch, *Social Preconditions for National Revival in Europe: A Comparative Analysis of the Social Composition of Patriotic Groups among the Smaller European Nations*, trans. Ben Fowkes (Cambridge and New York: Cambridge University Press, 1985).

30 See, for example, Geoffrey Hosking, *Russia: People and Empire, 1552–1917*, (London: HarperCollins, 1997).

31 Andreas Kappeler, *The Russian Empire: A Multiethnic History*, trans. Alfred Clayton (Harlow, England: Pearson Education, 2001).

32 Nathaniel Knight, "Ethnicity, Nationality, and the Masses: Narodnost' and Modernity in Imperial Russia," in *Russian Modernity: Politics, Knowledge, Practices*, eds. David Hoffmann and Yanni Kotsonis (London: Macmillan, 2000); Bassin, *Imperial Visions*, 38–41.

33 Greenfeld, *Nationalism*.

34 Astrid Tuminez, *Russian Nationalism since 1856: Ideology and the Making of Foreign Policy* (Lanham, MD: Rowman & Littlefield, 2000).

35 A very partial list of relevant sources would include Terry Martin, *Affirmative Action Empire: Nations and Nationalism in the Soviet Union, 1923–1939* (Ithaca, NY: Cornell University Press, 2001); Ronald Suny, *Revenge of the Past: Nationalism, Revolution, and the Collapse of the Soviet Union* (Stanford, CA: Stanford University Press, 1993); and Yuri Slezkine, "The USSR as a Communal Apartment, or How a Socialist State Promoted Ethnic Particularism," *Slavic Review* 53, no. 2 (1994): 414–53.

36 Stephen E. Hanson, *Time and Revolution: Marxism and the Design of Soviet Institutions* (Chapel Hill: University of North Carolina Press, 1997).

37 Joseph V. Stalin, *Marxism and the National Question* (New York: International Publishers, 1942).

38 For a fascinating empirical account of how early Soviet ethnographers arrived at and applied such categorical conclusions in practice, see Yuri Slezkine, *Arctic Mirrors: Russia and the Small Peoples of the North* (Ithaca, NY: Cornell University Press, 1994).

39 Indeed, one can persuasively analyze Stalin's own combination of formal, and rather consistent, Marxism-Leninism and his informal reliance (especially after 1938) on Russian cultural and historical symbolism to bolster his popular appeal, as a reflection of this tension. Certainly, to label Stalin a straightforward "Russian nationalist" is far too simple an understanding of his political belief system.

40 John Dunlop, *The Rise of Russia and the Fall of the Soviet Empire* (Princeton, NJ: Princeton University Press, 1993); Yitzhak Brudny, *Reinventing Russia: Russian Nationalism and the Soviet State, 1953–1991* (Cambridge, MA: Harvard University Press, 1998); Edward W. Walker, *Dissolution: Sovereignty and the Breakup of the Soviet Union* (Lanham, MD: Rowman & Littlefield, and Berkeley, CA: Berkeley Public Policy Press, 2003).

41 Aleksandr Solzhenitsyn, *Kak Nam Obustroit' Rossiiu: Posilnye Soobrazheniia* [How We Might Reconstruct Russia: Practical Suggestions] (Parizh, Russia: YMCA Press, 1990).

42 See, for example, Gennadii Ziuganov, *Derzhava* [Great Power] (Moscow: Informpechat', 1994). Ziuganov has articulated the themes of this treatise consistently since the founding of the Communist Party of the Russian Federation in 1990. For an excellent analysis of Ziuganov's ideas about the reconceptualization of Russia, see Veljko Vujacic, "Gennadiy Zyuganov and the 'Third Road,'" *Post-Soviet Affairs* 12, no. 2 (1996): 118–54.

43 While correctly emphasizing the political importance of Zhirinovskii's professed ideological beliefs, I myself missed the importance of the ironic aspects of his politics in my first published analysis of his party: Stephen E. Hanson, "Ideology, Uncertainty, and the Rise of Anti-System Parties in Post-Communist Russia," *Journal of Communist Studies and Transition Politics* 14, nos. 1–2 (1998): 98–127.

44 See, for example, Vladimir Zhirinovskii, *Poslednii Brosok Na Iug* (Moscow: TOO Pisatel': IK Bukvitsia, 1993).

45 "Putin's High Rating Confirmed by Polls," Interfax, November 18, 2005, reprinted at Johnson's Russia List (no. 9298), www.cdi.org/russia/johnson/default.cfm.

46 These are words I have personally heard Russians use countless times, remarkably consistently over the course of the post-Soviet period, in conversations about Zhirinovskii's appeal.

47 Stephen E. Hanson, "Instrumental Democracy: The End of Ideology and the Decline of Russian Political Parties," in *The 1999–2000 Elections in Russia: Their Impact and Legacy*, eds. Vicki L. Hesli and William M. Reisinger (Cambridge and New York: Cambridge University Press, 2003).

48 See, for example, Peter Lavelle's analysis in "The Poor Political Lexicon of Russia's Liberals," RIA-Novosti, September 26, 2005, accessed at http://en.rian.ru/analysis/20050926/41512468.html.

49 See Michael McFaul, "Vladimir Putin's Grand Strategy ... for Anti-Democratic Regime Change in Russia," *Weekly Standard*, November 17, 2003.

50 See, for example, Putin's 2000 interview about the Kremlin's decision to "exchange" journalist Andrei Babitsky for Russian military hostages held by the Chechens, in which he declared that Babitsky was not a "Russian journalist," since he failed to obey "the laws of his own country." In Vladimir Putin, Nataliya Gevorkyan, Natalya Timakova, and Andrei Kolesnikov, *First Person: An Astonishingly Frank Self-Portrait by Russia's President* (New York: PublicAffairs, 2000), 169–74.

51 Stephen E. Hanson, "On 'Double Standards': Toward Strategic Liberalism in U.S. Russia Policy," Policy Memo 368, Program on New Approaches to Russian Security (Washington, DC: Center for Strategic and International Studies, December 2005).

52 Vladimir Putin, quoted in Sergei Medvedev, "'Juicy Morsels': Putin's Beslan Address and the Construction of the New Russian Identity," Policy Memo 334, Program on New Approaches to Russian Security (Washington, DC: Center for Strategic and International Studies, November 2004).

53 See Igor Chubais' comments at "The Search for a New Russian Identity," Third Colloquium of the Russian Academy of Sciences Institute for World Economy and International Relations, Moscow, December 3, 1999, accessed at http://www.loc.gov/about/welcome/speeches/russianperspectives/colloq3s1.html.

PART TWO
INSTITUTIONAL CHANGE AND INTERACTIONS BETWEEN STATE AND SOCIETY

CHAPTER 4
PUBLIC DISCOURSE ON THE PERSPECTIVES ON TRANSITION IN POST-SOVIET RUSSIA: THE PLURALISM OF IDEAS IN TRANSFORMING THE PUBLIC SPHERE

OLGA MALINOVA

The spheres of public opinion and political communication in Russia have undergone unprecedented changes over the last 20 years. In contrast with the Soviet society dominated by "the only true" ideology, now many different political perspectives are publicly articulated without fear of persecution. The fact of ideological pluralism in post-Soviet Russia hardly raises doubts. But what are its political implications?

Theorists of democracy assume that freedom of expression is important not only as a basic human right but also as the fundamental condition of democratic rule. From the normative point of view, the "quality" of political communication might be evaluated by its capability to promote "enlightened understanding" among citizens (in Robert Dahl's terms[1]). Free expression of different programs gives people the opportunity to make up their minds about the whole spectrum of available political alternatives, which is particularly important for a society going through large-scale reforms. What matters is not only the opportunity to express different political views but also the effort to articulate more-or-less clear alternative visions of public problems whose competition could be a major factor in the shaping of public opinion. So, can we perceive in post-Soviet Russia any evidence of the development of a pluralist and democratic public sphere where such competing perspectives could be represented, criticized, and discussed? The current tendencies—the reduction of the number of places for public discussion as a result of political reforms by former President and now Prime Minister Vladimir Putin, and the expansion of a political "center" that tends to absorb a wide spectrum of positions without making clear distinctions among them—do not raise much optimism in this respect. But during the last 20 years, the vectors of transformation of the space where political ideas are produced, disseminated, and put into collision have changed more than once. So, to get the full picture, we need to analyze the entire course of this process. Unfortunately, the changes in the sphere of production and competition of social and political ideas in post-Soviet societies, which should be seen as an important aspect of these societies' transformation, did not receive much attention from "transitologists" in Russia and abroad. To a certain extent, this might be an effect of stereotypes based on the experience of Western countries: pluralism of political ideas is supposed to be a part of "the normal" democratic order that is ensured by freedom of thought and expression. So, it is presumed that the "infrastructure" for production and dissemination of ideas rises spontaneously; the only important thing is to provide freedom of expression and independence of the news media.

But in most Western countries, the basis of this infrastructure was formed under different social, cultural, and technical conditions. It was part of a certain type of public sphere in which indirect communications by means of print media were completed by immediate discussions and where the range of participants was limited to a small number of well-off, well-educated men who had enough time and skills for unhurried discussions on matters of public concern. This type of "bourgeois public sphere," as well as its role in the development of democratic order in Western countries, was well described by Jürgen Habermas.[2] The normative model elaborated by Habermas contributed greatly to critical development of the theory of democracy,[3] yet did not inform the study of democratic transitions very much.

However, the experience of Russia and some other post-communist countries gives evidence that the absence of censorship, a formal declaration of the freedom of expression, and at least the formal development of multiparty systems are essential but not sufficient conditions for making pluralism of political ideas "effective," that is, bringing society closer to the ideal of "enlightened understanding" among citizens. So, the changes that took place in post-Soviet Russia in the production and dissemination of social and political ideas deserve special study. These changes were not just a consequence of the transformation of social structures and political institutions but also an important factor that influenced this process.

There is considerable literature on the development of political ideologies in post-Soviet Russia. In the 1990s, many political scientists and historians studied the newly composed "complexes of ideas," trying to clear up the configuration of the emerging ideological spectrum. The most obvious way to understand the nascent trends was to correlate ideas articulated by politicians and public intellectuals with the major ideological traditions and to reveal the specific features of this or that "ism" in Russia. Usually such a process leads to the conclusion that there are many objective and subjective obstacles to the development of liberalism, conservatism, or social democracy (and to the growth of corresponding political movements).[4] In the mid-1990s, when President Boris Yeltsin declared the search for "the new national idea," many social scientists participated in its "invention," a process that also resulted in a stream of publications devoted to the perspectives of particular types of ideologies.

There were different opinions concerning the mechanisms of operation of "the new national idea." While some scholars argued that the desired "national idea" should become the new state ideology and set their hopes on a partial revival of former methods of ideological activity,[5] others were convinced that a new integrative ideology giving society "the language of symbols, values, and meanings" should be shaped by deliberate efforts of civic society.[6] The attempts to invent "the new national idea" (whatever was meant by this formulation) did not lead to any clear result. But the enthusiasm the scholars raised was strongly symptomatic: the lack of integrative projects on whose basis the new collective identities could be constructed in place of the lost ones was felt by many people. Somewhat more fruitful was a by-product of this enterprise: the discussion about "the national interests," which revealed a whole spectrum of positions on the topic that were useful for structuring public discussion.[7] In the 2000s, as a result of reforms of political institutions and politics initiated by President Putin in relation to mass media, the political landscape became more monotonous, and research interest in the political ideologies decreased somewhat, although some scholars still pay serious attention to this topic.[8]

The evolution of the space of political ideas in post-Soviet Russia is usually interpreted either as a consequence of regime transformation (which led at first to a pluralism of conflicting elites and goals, then to elimination of independent political actors and the appearance of a broad "center" that tries to absorb different sets of values) or in terms of the development of certain "isms" on "the Russian ground." Actually, there is one more explanation for the "deficiency" of production of political ideas that points to the irrelevance of "ideologies" in the modern society, where "ideas" are supplanted by "images" and political advertisement. The authors who offer this explanation feel doubts about the perspectives on the development of the space of political ideas in post-Soviet Russia and argue that the trend toward displacement of "ideology" by "imageology" reveals itself in Russia more bluntly than in mature democracies.[9] If they are right, t study political ideas means to spend time in vain. However, in my opinion this interpretation overestimates the weight of the new tendencies in political communication. The rise of "imageology" does not abolish the significance of "ideology"—we just deal now with more complex phenomena inasmuch as the dissemination of political ideas depends greatly on the way they are "packed" to compete with other commodities for the ear's attention.[10] "Ideas" are still relevant.

To my mind, all these approaches only partly explain a process that should be explored more comprehensively. To understand the transformation of the space of political ideas in post-Soviet Russia, we need to study not only ideas themselves but also the "environment" in which they are produced, confronted, justified, and contested. So, it makes sense to devote serious study to (1) the configuration of political ideas circulating in the public discourse, (2) institutional conditions that determine the strategies of political actors who produce these ideas, and (3) political communication that provides for the circulation of these ideas. To do this, we can appeal to the concept of the *public sphere*. Most often it is connected with the model of the "bourgeois public sphere" that was analyzed by Habermas in *The Structural Transformation of the Public Sphere*. He not only reconstructed a particular type of public sphere that appeared in bourgeois Europe in the 17th and 18th centuries and described its subsequent transformation, but also developed a normative model that provided important grounds for criticism and improvement of democratic practices. Consequently, the mainstream of works influenced by Habermas is focused on analysis of the gap between an ideal public sphere (that probably once existed) and the actual state of things in modern societies, where the aspiration for collective deliberation and active participation in public activity is lost. In this line of thinking, the concept of the public sphere is developed as a normative one related to some ideal model.

But this concept also could be understood in a descriptive way, and might be used for analysis of *different types of public spheres* that might not so closely resemble the ideal model. The work of Shmuel N. Eisenstadt and colleagues gives examples of this approach.[11] According to Eisenstadt and one such colleague, Wolfgang Schluchter,

> in every civilization with some complexity and literacy a public sphere will emerge, but not necessarily of the civil society type. It must be regarded as a sphere *between* the official and the private, and one that expands and shrinks according to the shifting involvement of the carrier strata that are not part of the rulership.[12]

In their interpretation, the notion of the public sphere points to some intermediate space between the private and official spheres where collective improvements (or the common good) are at stake. It is supposed that this space is not only relatively autonomous from the sphere of state administration but also more or less open to different segments of society. It might take the form of civic society (as in Western democracies), or not. According to Eisenstadt and Schluchter, "Public spheres tend to develop dynamics of their own, which, while closely related to that of the political arena, are not coterminous with it and are not governed by the dynamics of the latter."[13] The significance of the public sphere is partly determined by its institutional locus: for instance, whether it is heterogeneous or unified, concentrated in the center or inclusive of the periphery, or supposes interpretation of the public good before that of official or private people.

While the normative perspective could be useful for development of the concept of *democratization*, the descriptive approach to the study of the public sphere perfectly suits the concept of social *transformation*: it allows one to picture changing social structures by which political ideas are produced, disseminated, and put into collision in their own terms, analyzing what actually takes place. By no means do I reject the value of the normative approach, which is also applicable to the study of the post-Soviet public sphere.[14] In my opinion, the normative vision of the public sphere helps perfectly to explain what "is lacked," but it is not so helpful for explaining the process of transformation: the great difference between the ideal model and the actual state of things might obscure the real changes. Besides, we should admit that while in the context of criticism of practices of Western "real democracies" the normative approach to the public sphere is concentrated around the trope of nostalgia, in the post-Soviet context it nourishes the tropes of incompleteness and inferiority. Finally, even if transformation of the post-Soviet public sphere does not conform to the linear vector of "democratization," the changes still have been very great and deserve analysis.

To my mind, it makes sense to study the development of the space of political ideas in post-Soviet Russia as part of a wider process of transformation of the public sphere that might be seen *as the virtual space where socially significant issues are discussed, where public opinion takes shape, and where collective identities are defined and redefined*.[15] This space is constituted by a multitude of overlapping publics that have flexible temporal, spatial, and substantial borders; it is located in manifold institutions and depends greatly upon shifting involvement in public activity.[16] The transformation of the public space has a significant implication for changing interactions between the post-Soviet state and society as far as it means more-or-less radical modification of the ways of imagining society, formulating and discussing political aims, legitimizing new institutions, and constructing political identities. In the present chapter, I outline the major vectors of transformation of the public sphere in Russia from 1980 to the 2000s, pointing to

- *The institutional locus* of the public sphere (where the discussions about matters of public concern take place, as well as who can participate in them, and according to what rules).

- *The actors* of the public sphere (who produces the main concepts of the public good and why they do so, and what the goals and strategies of these actors are).

- *The watersheds* along which public political discourse is structured (what kinds of political ideas are the main competitors in the public arenas, or, alternately, are marginalized, being spread in fragmented counter–public spheres). Strictly speaking, the structure of public discourse is determined not only by the sides that are taken, but first of all by the issues that are discussed. For brevity's sake, I will concentrate on only one major issue that was at the center of public debate—the problem of perspectives on post-Soviet social and political transition—leaving aside many other important issues that have structured the field.

Of course, this will be just a bird's-eye view. It would be difficult to cover in one chapter all major aspects of the complex and contradictory process of transformation of the public sphere in such a large and diverse country as Russia over more than 20 years. Of necessity, an incomplete perspective "from the capital city" will be provided: even though the processes in different regions of Russia undoubtedly should be taken into consideration, they deserve special, substantive research. But I hope that this picture drawn with a broad brush might be useful to further detailed studies.

The starting point of my analysis is late Soviet society. Seemingly, the phrase "public sphere" with respect to the Soviet Union sounds like an oxymoron. Of course there was a developed system of institutions that intended to shape and articulate public opinion, but they were not autonomous from the official sphere. People who participated in public discourse were not free to express their thoughts (and in the worst times, they had to pay with their freedom and even their lives for "unhappy" statements). Finally, the discussions themselves were manipulated by officials.[17] Formally, the degree of involvement in this "official public sphere" was really great: practically every family subscribed to "central" newspapers and magazines, most of the territory of the Soviet Union was covered by television and radio broadcasting, and it would be accurate to assert that the "Soviet people, somewhat of their own will, [were] firmly rooted in the mass media and [could not] escape from getting a solid portion of official propaganda each day."[18] Besides, the greater part of the population was involved in the system of political education that was in a certain sense self-sustaining, insofar as it stimulated production of the great stream of indoctrinating literature that was used almost exclusively by its teachers and students. According to a calculation by Vladimir Shlapentokh, 12 to 14 million people (i.e., 10 percent of all employees) conducted ideological work on a daily basis in the framework of their profession, and no less than 8 million (this figure overlaps to some degree with the previous one) were involved in ideological work "after 5 o'clock." The two categories composed the majority of the socially active part of the Soviet population.[19] The mass participation in the campaigns of "public discussion" of certain principal laws (such as the constitution of 1977) or decisions of party congresses was not surprising. Of course, those campaigns were not causes for expression of actual feelings; rather, they were ritual actions for articulation of officially approved "opinions." That is why, according to the assessment of Yury Levada, "under the situation of demonstrative coercive 'like-mindedness,' the existence of public opinion in the modern sense of the term was impossible," insofar as individual opinions could not be independent.[20]

Nevertheless, late Soviet society should certainly be taken into consideration as the starting point if one wishes to follow the trajectory of contemporary transformation of the public sphere in Russia. First, the official discourse in the Soviet Union's later days was not monolithic: inside a single ideological framework (that by no means set certain limits), there were many different discourses. According to the joke, in the Soviet Union there was no pluralism of approaches (*podkhodov*), but there was a pluralism of entrances (*pod'ezdov*). (This was an allusion to variations in the discourses of the departments of the Communist Party Central Committee that were situated in the different "entrances" to a large building in the Old Square.) This "latent pluralism" still awaits a serious study.[21] Second, some institutes of the *official public sphere* (official and semiofficial public organizations, media, etc.), while under control of the Communist Party, still functioned as the channels of feedback, albeit very imperfectly.[22] And just for this reason, some of them got a fresh impulse at the time of perestroika. Third, the control of the state in late Soviet society was not all-embracing. In 1989, Vladimir Shlapentokh rightly pointed to a "privatization" of late Soviet society that was a result of two interconnected processes: "the radical decline in the authority of the state" and "the creation of civil society based on the private activity of the Soviet people."[23] Although the latter conclusion, in my opinion, is overbold, the tendency toward "privatization" and "fundamental individualization" of late Soviet society is also endorsed by other researchers.[24] The degree of this "privatization" should not be overestimated, inasmuch as the predominantly state-owned and state-administrated economy, as well as state/party control of various aspects of the life of individuals, limited the space in the private sphere, that is, for activity that, as Shlapentokh observed at the time, "is beyond systematic control by outside forces and presupposes both wide initiative on the part of its instigators and their right to communicate and cooperate with only those whom they like."[25] But some niches for this type of activity still appeared.

One implication of this tendency was the emergence of some nonofficial public space between the official sphere and the sphere of private life that Ingrid Osvald and Victor Voronkov have called the "public-private" sphere.[26] In late Soviet society, there was a whole system of institutions that constituted this "public-private" sphere: the distribution network for officially suppressed literature known variously as *samizdat* and *tamizdat*; "informal" (meaning not officially registered) organizations, from secret to semilegal; and, in a sense, kitchens, where people gathered with those whom they trusted to discuss problems of common concern. (Being situated in private places, kitchens were a unique locus for free discussions of public problems.) What was important was that these two public spheres were ruled by totally different sets of norms, which formed different patterns of behavior.[27] During their lives, Soviet people learned to distinguish carefully what they could discuss with family and friends, what they could say in official environments, and what could not be said at all. Of course, the space of the "public-private" sphere was exclusive (it was open only to those who merited credence) and fragmented. But, as Osvald and Voronkov have demonstrated, there were certain mechanisms that helped the "public-private" sphere get over this fragmentation—the culture of anecdotes, for example.[28] Discourses that significantly differed from the official versions intended "for mass use" also took place at "closed" or "half-closed" intellectual seminars for specialists (e.g., those who worked at the higher levels of the propaganda system, or researchers of the institutes of the Academy of Sciences). Thus, alongside the "public-private" sphere there also was *the "DSP" public sphere* (from the abbreviation indicating "for official use only," which marked one of the degrees of secrecy). So, it should be concluded that although there was no clear ideological pluralism in late Soviet society, it was not as monolithic as was officially supposed.

In the period of perestroika (1985–1991), the boundaries of the official, semiofficial, and unofficial public spheres became more and more permeable. On the one hand, the norms of the official public sphere changed with the introduction of glasnost, which was followed by timid attempts to develop intraparty democracy and finally by the reform of the political system. The new political opportunities arose inside certain "traditional" Soviet institutions: writers', cinematographers', and journalists' unions; the Academy of Sciences; and even some local organizations of the Communist Party and the national party youth group Komsomol. The democratization of these official public organizations was partly the result of their entitlement to appropriation of one-third of the seats of people's deputies of the Soviet Union in the late 1980s. This procedure revealed the undemocratic character of official organizations, but there was serious stimulus to use their benefits in the struggle for power.[29] On the other hand, the "public-private" sphere became not so private insofar as "informal organizations" (i.e., those not registered officially) were becoming more and more involved in the official political process, and the difference between the discourses in the kitchens and at the public meetings was becoming less and less perceptible.

The institutional locus of the *real public sphere* arose in areas of the mass media. At the beginning, the "discourse of perestroika," which increasingly went beyond the officially proclaimed slogans, was hosted by literary magazines (e.g., *Ogoniok, Novyi mir, Znamia, Oktiabr, Druzhba narodov*[30]) and newspapers (e.g., *Moscow News, Argumenty i fakty*). Later (1990–1991), it also appeared on the new radio and television channels. After the new law on regulation of the activity of mass media came into force (August 1, 1990), it became possible to set up independent media.

In the course of changes in the political system initiated by the Nineteenth Plenum of the Communist Party Central Committee (June 1988), some opportunities for public discussion appeared inside the political system itself. One of the results of the political reforms initiated by Mikhail Gorbachev was the creation of an important venue for the articulation of political ideas and opinions—the Congress of People's Deputies. Although the procedure for election to the Congress was nondemocratic, and its functions were largely ceremonial, the very existence of this institution generated significant public activity. Sessions of the Congress were broadcast on radio and television and drew great interest among citizens. (The impact was especially significant in May and June 1989, during the first session of the Congress.) Finally, there were a lot of places for immediate discussions, from occasional (and frequent) meetings to gatherings of regularly functioning political clubs and informal organizations.[31]

The circle of actors in the public sphere significantly widened. It was augmented not only by officials whose public behavior gradually altered under the influence of the new political style introduced by Gorbachev, but by members of traditional public organizations, artists' unions, informal organizations, and, beginning in 1990, by the new political parties and movements. Among the active participants in the public sphere were professionals—party officials, journalists, scientists, writers, artists, and cinematographers, among others—as well as ordinary citizens carried by the wave of political activity.

The aims, strategies, and norms of these actors also underwent some changes. If at the beginning of perestroika the main mission of politicians in the public sphere was to explain the "party line," and they could just hint at the nuances of their personal positions, then after 1990 it became possible to articulate different political programs openly. What was really important was that the mass political enthusiasm made political ideas a real weapon in the struggle for power. All of these developments strongly stimulated the production of ideas that were able to compete for the attention of the public.

The greatest role in shaping the public sphere in the period of perestroika was played by journalists. Up to the collapse of the Soviet Union and the beginning of economic reform in Russia, the only obstacle to journalists' activity was censorship. As the impact of political prohibitions diminished, the print media became the "fourth power," with increasing independence and influence, whereas the state power showed a growing ineffectiveness and the economy moved toward a state of chaos.[32] This new influence stimulated a specific professional ethos that had deep roots in the history of journalism in Russia. According to Ivan Zasurskii, most journalists "saw their task not in informing the public or shaping a reliable picture of reality, but in enlightenment, agitation, and organization of the masses for the sake of true aims and ideals."[33] Mass media played a decisive role in the spread of new ideologies that paved the way for subsequent political and economic transformations.

The public sphere in the period of perestroika was marked by a specific configuration of forms and channels of political communication. There was a real boom in the printed word that was fed by the intense face-to-face communications characteristic of the times. Newspapers, magazines, and literary works that were "taken off the tables" and published were closely read and vigorously discussed by a great number of people. Later, the same kind of attention was given to the broadcasts of independent television channels and radio stations. That made possible an unprecedented effect of integration of the public: many people all over the country read and discussed approximately the same corpus of texts, which quickly expanded but still remained "readable." It is not an overstatement to claim that the degree of integration of the audience in the period of perestroika was very close to the ideal model of the public sphere described by Habermas.

It should be mentioned, though, that this effect was the result of a very specific combination of circumstances. Paradoxically enough, active participation in public discussions was possible partly due to the preservation of socialist economics. The circulation of newspapers and magazines did not depend on their profit, and they were cheap enough. People had the opportunity to read and discuss the "deficit" press even during office time: the Soviet economic order in its later stages, though destroyed, still guaranteed stable salaries that depended not too strictly on productivity measures. Of course, everyday life became harder: there was a great shortage of essential goods, and keeping house took a lot of time. But in the words of Alfred O. Hirschman, in this period disappointment was "a ladder which [was used] to climb gradually out of the private life into the public arena."[34] With the beginning of economic reforms, active participation in public life became problematic for many people insofar as they had neither the time nor the means for it. Besides, the first results of these reforms did not support enthusiasm about the effectiveness of participation.

The perestroika years were a time when the ideological structure of Soviet society underwent quick and significant changes. First of all, these changes touched an official ideology. In 1985, the new political course started with the slogan "Let there be more socialism!" (*"Bol'she sotcializma!"*). The first buzzword was "acceleration" (*uskorenie*), soon to be replaced by "glasnost" (which supposed the necessity and opportunity to criticize the "defects" of socialism) and "the New Thinking." As early as 1987, the next new buzzword appeared—"perestroika" (meaning a removal of defects of the Soviet social order); added to it were the new slogans "Back to Lenin!" and "Let there be more democracy!" (*"Bol'she democratii!"*). At this stage, the repertoire of official ideology was extended by such "bourgeois" concepts as the Soviet rule of law (*sovetskoe pravovoe gosudarstvo*), parliamentarianism, the division of power, and human rights. The innovations were pushed by such "reformist" Communist Party ideologists as Alexander Iakovlev and quickly got theoretical grounds in the writings of specialists from research institutes of the Academy of Science and party think tanks.[35] To maintain continuity, these innovations were introduced under the cover of a "return to the true socialism." According to the memoirs of one of the members of Gorbachev's staff, "When there were no ready phrases by Lenin for justification of this or that action, Gorbachev, with no confusion, invented his own. The most important thing was to supply any unorthodox term with the calming definition 'the socialist.'"[36] The official ideology thus made an evident drift toward democratic socialism.[37] The whole "ideological apparatus" was used for propagation of these ideas. But the changes were too radical and too quick; the official commentaries on the new party documents were not always ready in time. So, as I remember from my own short experience of lecturing in the system of political education (during 1987–1988), sometimes propagandists had to apply their professional skills and invent their own comments (which itself was a distortion of the canon). As Irina Chechel has written, "The ideological vertical became dispersed to many centers."[38] Orthodoxy was breaking apart not only because of the challenges from the outside (i.e., competing ideas and concepts), but also as a result of dissolution of the once-centralized system of its translation.

The changes in official ideology provoked opposition from radicals and conservatives alike.[39] The former developed a loose, although distinctive, set of ideas that has been called "the basic democratic ideology."[40] These ideas were articulated by "perestroika periodicals" (*perestroehnye izdaniia*) and shared by many informal movements; later, they formed the basis of an ideology of newly created political parties identifying themselves as "democrats." This "basic democratic ideology" regarded the Soviet "totalitarian" system as a "deviation" from "the normal" way of social evolution. The destruction of this system was thus seen as the first step toward "normality." In the context of the collapse of economics and the crisis of the political system, this set of ideas little by little won the dominant positions.

But "basic democratic ideology" was not the only opposition ideology: there were two other alternatives to the changing official course. The first was orthodox communism: the adherents to this alternative did not regard the Soviet system as defective and saw the politics of Gorbachev as a betrayal of communist ideals. This opposition was strong enough both at the official level (in the Central Party Committee, it was represented by Egor Ligachev, a longtime member of the old guard) and at "informal" levels (at the end of 1988, some "informal" communist organizations were created). The other alternative was nationalism (or patriotism)—an ideology that had roots both in the dissident movement and in the circles of Soviet intellectuals gathered around the magazines *Molodaia gvardia* (Young guard) and *Nash sovremennik* (Our contemporary). During the time of perestroika, ideas of this type did not win wide popularity: being critical of the Western experience, they were not "opposed enough" to the Soviet system. Consequently, the main ideological watershed in the time of perestroika was the assessment of the Soviet system and of its antipode—Western capitalism. The development of the real public sphere supported by actual mass participation created favorable conditions for the rise in popularity of more radical versions of critical concepts.

With the collapse of the Soviet Union and the beginning of economic reforms in Russia, the public sphere entered a new phase. Summarizing the period (1991–1999), I shall describe it as Yeltsin's time, although it would be correct to make some differentiations within it (the most important being the beginning of the war in Chechnya and Yeltsin's second presidential campaign). The institutional locus of the public sphere remained formally the same—namely, the mass media—but the comparative importance of the institutions that composed it changed noticeably. The other significant site for articulation of political ideas became the parliament (whose structure and place in the political system were changed principally by the constitution adopted in 1993).[41] With the decrease in mass political activity, the communication sites that supported face-to-face public discussions became more specialized, and more oriented toward particular political organizations or professional groups. The traditional channels of public communication were augmented by the Internet, whose role, starting in the second half of the 1990s, became increasingly evident.[42] Among the principal actors of the public sphere were officials and public politicians, party activists, journalists, and experts; but starting in the mid-1990s, a more decisive role in political communication was played by political consultants and public relations agencies (both of which contributed greatly to the results of the presidential elections of 1996).

So, the list of "places" where public discourse occurred, as well as the circle of its participants, had not changed much since the end of the 1980s, with the critical exception of cyberspace. But these places' comparative significance—as well as the rules and strategies that influenced the behavior of those who produced, spread, and contested political ideas—changed greatly.

First of all, in regard to the mass media, with the beginning of economic reforms in 1992 the press faced a quick rise in the prices of paper, printing, and delivery. These problems were increased by the shrinkage of markets caused by the collapse of the Soviet Union. So, the periodicals—many of which had once called for market reforms—very quickly felt the effects of economic innovation on their own budgets. Forced to survive, they met this task in different ways: some sought state subventions; others tried to get private donations (in 1990, politicized private capital willingly though not evenly invested in mass media) or became part of commercial holdings.[43] The economic problems (which were experienced not only by the newspapers, but also by their readers) initiated the process of fragmentation of the audience for national periodicals, and then the reduction of their circulation and influence.

One segment of the print media that prospered in the early 1990s consisted of regional and local publications. They experienced a rapid rise in circulation in large part because, in comparison with the all-Russia periodicals, they were closer to the needs of their readers (the period of abstract political rhetoric was over) and less expensive, insofar as their delivery prices were lower. According to Liudmila Resnianskaia and Irina Fomicheva, in 1991 the all-Russia periodicals had made up three-fourths of total circulation; by 1997, the same share belonged to regional and local papers.[44] This meant a quick regionalization of press markets and partial disintegration of a formerly unified media system. Also, while in the 1980s the audiences for the all-Russia press and local and regional press had overlapped by approximately 80 percent, by the middle of the 1990s this overlap had decreased to less than 50 percent.[45] By the end of the decade, the total audience of the national newspapers was no more that 20 percent of the population.[46]

This collapse of readership levels of national periodicals meant a dramatic change in the structure of political communication: the audience for periodicals not only radically decreased, it also became fragmented. Starting in 1992, the closest thing to a unified source of national information was television. This happened because Russia had inherited from the Soviet Union a system of nationwide television broadcasting that covered almost the entire Russian territory. Because of the relatively low cost of watching television, many people substituted it for reading newspapers. This process had serious implications for the transformation of the public sphere: the logic of audiovisual communication dictates its own rules, subjecting the presentation of information to many of the requirements of entertainment. The specialists who study the evolution of television in post-Soviet Russia verify a clear drift in this direction.[47] The genre of political discussions on television, very popular during 1990–1996, later was increasingly supplanted by entertainment broadcasting and suffered from the growing availability and popularity of video games and other forms of leisure-use computer software. (This tendency became even more noticeable in the Putin period.)

In any event, in the 1990s television played a determining role in the production of political meaning and structuring of the ideological spectrum. Being the main channel of political communication on a national level, it became an object of struggle between political and financial groups. According to some scholars, the large commercial media holdings (such as Vladimir Gusinskii's Media-Most, the components of the state mass media that by the end of 1990s were controlled by Boris Berezovskii, and the group of mass media outlets patronized by the mayor of Moscow, Yury Luzhkov) fulfilled some of the functions of political parties, such as articulating certain systems of political beliefs and cultural paradigms. As Ivan Zasurskii has said, "TV channels were the real parties. It was they who played a political performance and developed a hierarchy of roles ... that later, before elections, were converted into the brands of political parties and movements for which the constituency was to vote."[48]

As a result of these tendencies, the professional norms and strategies of journalists became much more diverse in comparison with previous periods. As Alexander Kustarev has demonstrated, many professional conflicts have grown out of the economic, cultural, and political circumstances under which the mass media operated in post-Soviet Russia.[49] The "golden age" of the Russian mass media, with their ideology of their mission as the "fourth" power, called to educate the public, was now in the past. Political ideas became a commodity whose production and dissemination depended on the changing state of the market. Nevertheless, until the middle of the

1990s, some national mass media outlets remained relatively independent players in the public sphere (an example of this being their opposition to the first Chechen war).

The motives of the other major producer of ideologies—the members of the "political class"—also changed. The rules of formation and performance of the Russian parliament and government that were adopted after 1993, as well as the division of power between them, did not stimulate the political parties—the principal providers of competing programs—to fulfill this function as far as the political course was determined by the president (who was not affiliated with any party). Because of this, as well as some other circumstances,[50] most of the Russian parties preferred to fight for votes by means not of "ideology" but of "imageology." Of course, there also were some "ideological" parties that based their collective identity on certain types of ideology (the clearest examples being the Communist Party of the Russian Federation and several liberal parties). But these parties' constituents were concentrated in limited segments, and in the 1990s and 2000s they steadily lost positions from one federal election to the next.

The structure of the field of political ideas was determined by the polarization of the political spectrum, which became especially obvious in the mid-1990s. The dominant place in the space of public political discussion was occupied by the principal opponents—a group of parties that could be characterized generally as "democrats," and the Communist Party and its allies. The ideologies of the "democrats" arose in the process of development and diversification of "the basic democratic ideology." Its main proponents were the major liberal parties—Democratic Choice of Russia and Yabloko[51]—as well as some of the mass media, mainly the television channel NTV and other outlets that were holdings of Media-Most. More-or-less systematic versions of liberal ideology were produced and disseminated via limited party channels (such as brochures and irregularly published low-circulation newspapers). But some basic elements of "the basic democratic ideology" were loosely used in the rhetoric of state officials and in the programs of "centrist" parties (such as Nash Dom—Rossiia) that provided at least an opportunity for the ideology to be recognized by a wider audience. In the center of this kind of ideology was the idea of reforms that would make Russia "a normal civilized country" (the West was more or less explicitly seen as the standard) with a market economy, private property, and democratic political institutions. The concrete design of these reforms was seen in different ways; the particular point of disagreement and political demarcation was the attitude toward the actual course of reforms started by the government of Yegor Gaidar, who became acting prime minister in 1992.

The Communists presented themselves as uncompromising opponents of the "regime of national betrayal." There were various versions of the communist ideology.[52] The most "successful" of them (according to election results) was represented by the Communist Party of the Russian Federation and its allies in the National-Patriotic bloc. The party combined traditional communist rhetoric with criticism of liberalism and Westernism, and included some elements of Russian nationalism of the imperial type. The Communists' ideology was produced and disseminated mostly through party channels (although it should be mentioned that the number of members of this network was much larger than any of the liberal parties could boast). It had fewer opportunities to be represented to a broader audience via television channels, but it was not totally neglected by the national mass media: the Communists were considered the principal opposing force, and their activities were covered regularly though not neutrally.

Of course, the opposition of "democrats" and "Communists" did not exhaust the range of ideological watersheds in Yeltsin's Russia. During this long period, there were a lot of issues that divided society along different cleavages. But the problem of the perspectives on reform was at the center, and controversy between "democrats" and "Communists" noticeably dominated the field of political debate. That led to a relative marginalization of the other "producers" of political ideas.

On the whole, the public sphere of the Yeltsin period might be characterized as *pluralism in conflict*. There was a sharp struggle for public opinion in which many actors took part, and the fourth power did not strive to become the only player on this field (although it did not hesitate to use its resources for pressure; the struggle by no means was equal in this sense).

The vectors of transformation of the public sphere obviously changed when Vladimir Putin came to office. Formally, the institutional locus of the public sphere remained the same; so did that of its principal actors, though their roles changed substantially. The new regime tended to introduce "monocentrism" (Alexey Zudin's term[53]), that is, it either excluded or marginalized the players it could not control. As a result of political reforms initiated by Putin, the fields where alternative political projects could be articulated and contested had converged. The ideological landscape also altered greatly: the dominant role now belonged to an ever-expanding "center" that pretended to a "synthetic" and highly eclectic ideology absorbing various positions without clear differentiations among them. Such a strategy is very good in the struggle for support of the electorate, but it becomes realizable only when the other "producers" of political ideas and symbols both from the right and the left are too weak to counter it.

At the same time the authority demonstrates its allegiance to pluralism, at least in words, it tries to stimulate from above the development of political parties, and even creates some new institutions for representation (or the imitation of representation) of public opinion. (The last project of this type is formation of the "public chamber.") Consequently, pluralism in the public sphere is not prohibited, and the alternative discourses are not so much restricted as marginalized. At the same time, the fragmentation of the public increases. Along with the "main" public sphere that becomes more and more an *official* one,[54] there arise many alternative and marginalized public spheres that unite the publics composed of like-minded persons who do not have access to the principal channels for translation of opinions beyond their own circles.

This description is only a short sketch that provides an opportunity to assess the main trends in the transformation of the post-Soviet public sphere in Russia. Nevertheless, it shows that the production, dissemination, and competition of political ideas all deserve certain institutional conditions, as well as actors who are motivated to participate in these kinds of activity. Changes in these conditions lead to modification of the structure of public discourse and political communication. But the character of ideas competing in the public sphere is also very important from the perspective of institutional development.

The trajectory of the transformation of the public sphere in post-Soviet Russia can be summarized in the following way: from (1) dualism of official and unofficial public spheres in the late stages of the Soviet Union to formation of the "real" public sphere during the period of perestroika, as a result of the erosion of boundaries between the official sphere and the "private-public" sphere (as well as the "DSP" public sphere), to (2) the conflict pluralism in the public sphere in the mid-1990s, to (3) a "monocentric" public sphere dominated by loose official ideology with pluralism "at the margins," as the new century (and the Putin era) began. Of course, this scheme merits greater elaboration. And there are many related questions that must be answered. But those are matters for further research.

NOTES

1   Robert A. Dahl, *Democracy and Its Critics* (New Haven, CT: Yale University Press, 1989), 111.

2   Jürgen Habermas, *The Structural Transformation of the Public Sphere: An Inquiry into a Category of Bourgeois Society* (Cambridge, MA: MIT Press, 1993).

3   See Craig Calhoun, ed., *Habermas and the Public Sphere* (Cambridge, MA: MIT Press, 1992); Nick Crossley and John Michael Roberts, eds., *After Habermas: New Perspectives on the Public Sphere* (Oxford and Malden, MA: Blackwell, 2004); John M. Roberts, *The Aesthetics of Free Speech: Rethinking the Public Sphere* (New York: Macmillan, 2003).

4   S.V. Alekseev, V.A. Kalymanov, and A.G. Chernenko, *Ideologicheskie Orientiry Rossii* [Ideological Key Points of Russia], 2 vols. (Moscow: Kniga I biznes, 1998); Andrey Andreev, *Politicheskii Spektr Rossii: Structury, Ideologii, Osnovnye Sub'ekty* [Russia's Political Spectrum: Structure, Ideology, and the Main Actors] (Moscow: Editirial URSS, 1997); S.L. Gostev, "Obschestvenno-Politicheskie Organizatcii Radikal'no-Natcionalisticheskogo Tolka: Ih Elektorat i Rol' v Sovremennom Politicheskom Processe" [Public Political Organizations of the Radical Nationalist Type: Their Electoral Role in the Contemporary Political Process], *Vestnik Moskovskogo Universiteta* [Moscow University Messenger] 12, no. 2 (1999); V. Golovin, "Social-Demokratia v Razvityh Stranah i v Rossii (Social'no-Economicheskie Aspekty)" [Social Democracy in Developed Countries and in Russia (Social and Economic Aspects], in *Social-democratia v Evrope na poroge XXI veka* [Social Democracy on the Eve of the Twenty-First Century] (Moscow: INION RAN, 1998); Vladimir A. Gusev, "Stanovlenie Tret'ei Volny Russkogo Konservatizma (Nachalo 1990-h gg.)" [The Establishment of the Third Wave of the Russian Conservatism (Early 1990s], *Vestnik Moskovskogo Universiteta* [Moscow University Messenger] 12, no. 6 (1999); Olga Yu. Malinova, *Liberalism v Politicheskom Spektre Rossii*. (*Na Primere Partii "Democraticheskii vybor Rossii" i Obschestvennogo Ob'edinenia "Yabloko"*) [Liberalism in the Russian Political Spectrum (Case Study of "Democratic Choice of Russia" and "Yabloko"] (Moscow: Pamiatniki Istoricheskoi Mysli, 1998); I.V. Pruss, "Ryvok v Buduschee ili Dvizhenie po Krugu? (Economicheskie Vzgliady Sovremennyh Russkih Natcionalistov)" [Jumping into to the Future or Running Around in Circles? (Economic Ideas of the Modern Russian Nationalists)], *Polis no. 3* (1997); Vladimir V. Sogrin, "Liberalism v Rossii: Peripetii i Perspectivy" [Liberalism in Russia: Directions and Perspectives], *Obschestvennye Nauki i Sovremennost'* [Social Sciences and Modern Times] no. 1 (1997); Valerii D. Solovei, "Natsional-Radikalism" [National Radicalism], in *Politicheskie Partii Rossii: Istoria i Sovremennost'* [Russian Political Parties: History and Modernity], eds. Valentin Shelokhaev, et al. (Moscow: ROSSPEN, 2000), 594–621; Marina R. Kholmskaia, *Kommunisty Rossii: Fakty, Idei, Tendentcii* (Informatcionno-Analiticheskii Obzor) [Russian Communists: Facts, Ideas, Tendencies] (Moscow: Partinform, 1998).

5   Yury G. Volkov, "Ideologia v Zhizni Sovremennogo Rossiiskogo Obschestva" [Ideology in the Life of Contemporary Society], *Sotcial'no-Gumanitarnye Znania* [Social and Humanitarian Knowledge] no. 6 (1999); Andranik M. Migranian, Aleksei F. Elymanov, and Valerii D. Solovei, "Opyty Gosudarstvennoi Ideologii v Sovremennoi Rossii" [The

Practice of State Ideology in Modern Russia], in *Rossia: Poisk Puti* [Russia: The Search for the Way] (Moscow: Nauchnaia kniga, 1999); "Formirovanie Novoi Rossiiskoi Ideologii. Materialy Kruglogo Stola" [Shaping the New Russian Ideology], *Svobodnaia Mysl'* [Free Thought] 2000, no. 3, 4.

6   Tatiana A. Alekseeva, Boris G. Kapustin, and Igor' K. Pantin, "Perspektivy Integrativnoi Ideologii (Tezisy)" [Perspectives of Integrative Ideology (Propositions)] *Polis* no. 3 (1997): 18; Boris G. Kapustin, "Ideologii Sovremennoi Rossii: Poisk Modal'nosti Sopriazheniia" [Ideologies of Modern Russia: In Search of the Mode of Conjunction], *Etika Uspekha* [Ethics of Success] 7 (1996): 63–66.

7   See the analysis of this discussion in Boris Mezhuev, "Poniatie 'Natsional'nyi Interes' v Rossiiskoi Obschestvenno-Politicheskoi Mysli" [The Concept of "National Interest" in Russian Public and Political Thought], *Polis* no. 1 (1997): 5–31, and Alexander V. Fediakin, "Sovremennye Obschestvenno-Politicheskie Discussii o Natsional'nykh Interesakh Rossii" [Contemporary Public and Political Discussions about Russian National Interests], *Vestnik Moskovskogo universiteta* 12, no. 1 (2001): 30–45.

8   Victor A. Schnirel'man, *Intellektual'nye Labirinty: Ocherki Ideologii Sovremennoi Rossii* [Intellectual Labyrinths: Essays about Ideology in Modern Russia] (Moscow: Academia, 2004); Grigory V. Golosov and Yulia D. Shevchenko, "Globalizatciia i Antiglobalism v Politicheskoi Zhizni Rossii" [Globalization and Antiglobalism in Russian Political Life], in *Vlast' i Elity v Sovremennoi Rossii* [Power and Elites in Modern Russia], ed. Alexander Duka (St. Petersburg: Sotciologicheskoe Obschestvo im. Kovalevskogo, 2003), 399–412; Mikhail M. Sokolov, "Klassovoe kak Etnicheskoe: Ritorika Russkogo Radikal'no-Natcionalisticheskogo Dvizheniia" [Class as Ethnicity: Rhetoric of the Russian Radical-Nationalist Movement], *Polis* no. 2 (2005): 127–37.

9   See Susanna N. Pshizova, "Demokratiia i Politicheskii Rynok v Sravnitel'noi Perspective" [Democracy and Political Markets in Comparative Perspective], *Polis* no. 2 (2000): 3; and Alexander I. Soloviev, "Politicheskaia Ideologia: Logika Istoricheskoi Evoliutcii" [Political Ideology: The logic of Historical Evolution], *Polis* no. 2 (2001): .

10   See Olga Yu. Malinova, Doklad na seminare "Sovremennye Tendentcii Razvitia Simvolicheskogo Prostranstva Politiki i Concept Ideologii" [Paper presented at seminar, "Contemporary Tendencies in the Development of Symbols in Politics and the Concept of Ideology], *Polis* no. 4 (2004): 37–42.

11   Shmuel N. Eisenstadt, Wolfgang Schluchter, and Björn Wittrock, eds., *Public Spheres and Collective Identities* (New Brunswick, NJ, and London: Transaction Publishers, 2001); Miriam Hoexter, Shmuel N. Eisenstadt, and Nehemia Levtzion, eds., *The Public Sphere in Muslim Societies* (Albany: State University of New York, with the Van Leer Jerusalem Institute, Jerusalem, 2002).

12   Shmuel N. Eisenstadt and Wolfgang Schluchter, "Introduction: Path to Early Modernities—A Comparative View," in Eisenstadt et al., *Public Spheres and Collective Identities*, 12.

13   Ibid., 11.

14   See Yury A. Krasin, "Publichnaia Sfera i Publichnaia Politika v Rossiiskom Izmerenii" [Russian Dimensions of Public Sphere and Public Policy], in *Publichnaia Politika v Rossii: Po Itogam Proekta "Universitet Kalgari–Gorbachev-Fond* [Public Policy in Russia: Results of the Calgary University and Gorbachev-Fond Project], ed. A. Krasin (Moscow: Alpina Business Books, 2005), 18–25; Yasen N. Zasurshii, "Zhurnalistika i Obschetvo: Balansiruia Mezhdu Gosudarstvom, Bisnesom i Obschestvennoi Sferoi" [Journalism and Society: Keeping Balance Among State, Business, and Public Spheres], in *Sredstva Massovoi*

Informatsii Postsovetskoi Rossii [Mass Media in Post-Soviet Russia], ed. Ya.N. Zasurskogo (Moscow: Aspect-Press, 2002), 196–98.

15 This definition follows the interpretations that are usual for the Western (particularly the Habermasian) tradition. In Russian literature, the term "public sphere" has not yet achieved wide circulation. As the discussion published in the magazine *Sotcial'nye issledovania* has demonstrated, there is no convenient definition of this term among Russian social scientists. See Yury A. Krasin and Yulia M. Rosanova, "Publichnaia Sfera i Gosudarstvennaia Publichnaia Politika v Sovremennoi Rossii" (Public Sphere and State Public Policy in Contemporary Russia], *Sotciologicheskie issledovaniia* no. 10 (2000): 85–87). Yury Krasin, who has worked with the concept of the public sphere the most explicitly, prefers to use it in a broader sense, including in the public sphere not just "communication between citizens and public reflection" but also "practical actions for public good." See Krasin, "Publichnaia Sfera i Publichnaia Politika," 18–21.

16 Albert O. Hirschman had demonstrated that an intuitive feeling that "our societies are in some way predisposed towards oscillations between periods of intense preoccupation with public issues and of almost total concentration on individual improvement and private welfare goals" has some basis in cyclical factors affecting the transformation of preferences of masses of people. Hirschman, *Shifting Involvements: Private Interest and Public Action* (Princeton, NJ: Princeton University Press, 2002), 3.

17 Readers who have had no experience in dealing with this "official public sphere" may get a notion of it from Vladimir Shlapentokh, *Public and Private Life of the Soviet People: Changing Values in Post-Stalin Russia* (New York and Oxford: Oxford University Press, 1989): 95–138.

18 Ibid., 104.

19 Ibid., 106.

20 Yury Levada, *Ot Mnenii k Ponimaniiu: Sotciologicheskie Ocherki 1993–2000* [From Opinion to Understanding: Sociological Essays 1993–2000] (Moscow: Moskovskaia Shkola Politicheskih Issledovanii, 2000), 15.

21 A significant contribution to it is a book by Nikolai Mitrokhin about the Russian nationalist movement in the Soviet Union. One of the chapters describes the influence of the Communist Party Central Committee on the development of Russian nationalism. Mitrokhin, *Russkaia Rartiia: Dvizhenie Russkikh Natsionalistov v SSSR 1953–1985 Gody* [The Russian Party: The Movement of Russian Nationalists in the USSR, 1953–1985] (Moscow: Novoe Literaturnoe Obozrenie, 2003).

22 Alexander Sungurov, *Funktcii Politicheskoi Sistemy: ot Zastoia k Perestroike/Prilozhenie k Zhurnaly "Severnaia Pal'mira"* [The Functions of the Political System: From Stagnation to Perestroika] (St. Petersburg: SPb. Center "Strategy", 1998), 24–26, 38–40.

23 Shlapentokh, *Public and Private Life of the Soviet People*, 227.

24 See A.A. Golov and Yu.A. Levada, Sovetskii prostoi chelovek. *Opyt sotcial'nogo portreta na rubezhe 1990-h* [The Average Soviet Person: An Attempt at A Social Portrait At the Turn of the Century] (Moscow: Mirovoi okean, 1993); Oleg V. Kharhordin, *Oblichat' I litcemerit': genealogiia rossiiskoi lichnosti* [To Blame and to Dissemble: The Genealogy of the Russian Personality] (St. Petersburg: Evropeiskii Universitet v Sankt-Peterburge, Letnii sad, 2002).

25 Shlapentokh, *Public and Private Life of the Soviet People*, 4.

26 Ingrid Osvald and Viktor Voronkov, "The 'Public-Private' Sphere in Soviet and Post-Soviet Society: Perception and Dynamic of 'Public' and 'Private' in Contemporary Russia," *European Societies* 6 (2004): 97–117.

27 Yury Levada and his colleagues consider "double-mindedness" (*"dvoemyslie"*) one of the principal socio-anthropological characteristics of "Homo sovieticus" (Levada, *Ot Mnenii k Ponimaniiu*, 17).

28 Osvald and Voronkov, "The 'Public-Private' Sphere in Soviet and Post-Soviet Society," 110.

29 Sungurov, *Funktcii Politicheskoi Sistemy*, 103–105, 115–37.

30 At the end of 1980s, the circulation of these magazines increased three to four times; it became comparable with the circulation of many newspapers.

31 The history of one such political club—Perestroika, in St. Petersburg—was described by Alexander Sungurov in *Et'udy Politicheskoi Zhizni Leningrada-Peterburga: 1987–1994 gg./Prilozhenie k zhurnaly "Severnaia Pal'mira"* [Sketches of Political Life in Leningrad–St. Petersburg—Supplement to the Magazine "Severnaia Pal'mira"] (1996), 9–47.

32 Ivan Zasurskii, *Mass-Media Vtoroi Respubliki* [Mass Media of the Second Republic] (Moscow: Izdatel'stvo Moskovskogo Universiteta, 1999), 58.

33 Ibid., 54. Alexander Kustarev mentions that "the interpretation of journalism in terms of moral service was a distinctive feature of the business ethics of Soviet journalists" ("Konkurentciia i konflikt v zhurnalistike" [Competition and Conflict in Journalism], *Pro et Contra* 5, no .4 (2000), 9. Actually, this vision of the profession of journalism is deeply rooted in the traditions of 19th-century Russian literature. It should not be interpreted as something exclusively Russian, though: the ethos of enlightenment and education of the masses was typical of many modernizing countries. Of course, it must come into conflict with the new sets of norms arriving with market economies.

34 Hirschman, *Shifting Involvements*, 65–66.

35 The authorship of these innovation-oriented works sometimes can be established by the memoirs of contemporaries. Research by Robert Herman based on a series of interviews with experts in international relations throws some light on the interests and ideas that lay in the background of the concept of "the New Thinking." See Robert Herman, "Identity, Norms, and National Security: The Soviet Foreign Policy Revolution and the End of the Cold War," in *The Culture of National Security: Norms and Identity in World Politics*, ed. Peter J. Katzenstein (New York: Columbia University Press, 1996): 271–316.

36 Alexey Grachev, *Gorbachev* (Moscow: Vagrius, 2001), 148–49.

37 See Vladimir V. Sogrin, *Politicheskaia Istoriia Sovremennoi Rossii, 1985–2001: ot Gorbacheva do Putina* [Political History of Contemporary Russia, 1985–2001: From Gorbachev to Putin] (Moscow: Ves' Mir, 2001): chapters 1–4.

38 Irina Chechel, "Issledovanie Sovremennoi Intellektual'noi Istorii: Sovetskoe Obschestvennoe soznanie 1985–1991" [The Study of Contemporary Intellectual History: Soviet Public Consciousness, 1985–1991], in *Gorbachevskie chteniia: Stanovlenie Democratii v Sovremennoi Rossii: Ot Gobracheva do Putina: Perestroika 20 let spustiia: Vzgliad Molodykh Issledovatelei* [The Gorbachev Readings. Establishing Democracy in Modern Russia: From Gorbachev to Putin—Twenty Years after Perestroika: A View by Young Scholars], ed. O.M. Zdravomyslova (Moscow: Gorbachev Fund, 2004), 161.

39 The first manifestation of radical opposition was the statement by Yeltsin at the Plenum of the Central Committee (October 1987). The conservative opposition set forth its ideas in an article by Nina Andreeva, "Ne Mogu Postupit'sia Printcipami" [I Cannot Give Up Principles], published in the newspaper *Sovetskaia Rossiia* in March 1988.

40 Grigory Golosov, "Proishozhdenie Sovremennyh Rossiiskih Politicheskih Partii, 1987–1993" [Genealogy of Contemporary Russian Parties], in *Pervyi Electoral'nyi Tsikl v Rossii (1993–1996)* [The First Electoral Cycle in Russia (1993–1996)], eds. Vladimir

Gel'man, Grigory Golosov, and Elena Meleshkina (Moscow: Ves' Mir, 2000), 79–80.

41 For research on the Russian parliament in 1989 through 1993, see Nikolai Biryukov and Victor Segeev, *Russia's Road to Democracy: Parliament, Communism and Traditional Culture* (Aldershot, England: Edward Elgar, 1993); and Viktor L. Sheinis, *Vzlet i Padenie Parlamenta: Perelomnye Gody v Rossiiskoi Politike* (1985–1993) [The Rise and Fall of Parliament: The Years of Change in Russian Politics (1985–1993)], 2 vols. (Moscow: Carnegie Moscow Center; Fond INDEM, 2005).

42 On the role of the Internet in political communication in Russia, see Boris V. Ovchinnikov, "Virtual'nye Nadezhdy: Sostoianie i Perspektivy Politicheskogo Runeta" [Virtual Hopes: The State and Perspectives of Political Runeta], Polis no. 1 (2002): 46–65; and Dmitry N. Peskov, "Internet v Rossiiskoi Politike: Utopia i Real'nost" [The Internet in Russian Politics: Utopia and Reality], *Polis* no. 1 (2002): 31–45.

43 Zasurskii, *Mass-Media Vtoroi Respubliki*, chapter 2.

44 Liudmila L. Resnianskaia and Irina D. Fomicheva, *Gazeta dlia vsei Rossii* [The Newspaper for All of Russia] (Moscow: IKAR, 1999), 14.

45 Ibid., 58. The development of regional public spheres is a special question that I will not touch upon here.

46 Elena Vartanova, "Media v post-sovetskoi Rossii: ih struktura i vliianie" [The Media in Post-Soviet Russia: Structure and Influence], *Pro et Contra* 5, no. 4 (2000), 64.

47 See, for example, Boris Dubin, "Ot initciativnyh grupp k anonimnym media: massovye kommunikatcii v rossiiskom obschestve" [From Initiative Groups to Anonymous Media: Mass Communications in Contemporary Russian Society], *Pro et Contra* 5, no. 4 (2000): 31–60.

48 Ivan Zasurskii, "SMI I vlast'. Rossiia devianostyh" [Media and Power in 1990s Russia], *Sredstva massovoi informatsii postsovetskoi Rossii* [Media of Post-Soviet Russia], (New York : M.E. Sharpe, 2004) 98–99.

49 Kustarev, "Konkurentciia i konflikt v zhurnalistike."

50 See Olga Malinova, "Partiinye ideologii v Rossii: atribut ili anturazh" [Party Ideologies in Contemporary Russia: Attribute or Entourage], *Polis* no. 5 (2001): 97–106.

51 Vladimir V. Sogrin, "Liberalism v Rossii: peripetii i perspektivy" [Liberalism in Russia: Directions and Perspectives], *Obschestvennye nauki i sovremennost'* no. 1 (1997): 13–23; and Malinova, *Liberalism v politicheskom spektre Rossii*.

52 For an analysis of communist ideologies in the 1990s, see Kholmskaia, *Kommunisty Rossii: Fakty, Idei, Tendetcii* [Russia's Communists: Facts, Ideas, Tendencies] and Boris G. Kapustin, "Levyi Konservatizm KPRF I Ego rol'v Sovremennoi Politike" [The Left Conservatism of the Communist Party of the Russian Federation], in Kapustin, *Ideologiia i Politika v Postkommunisticheskoi Rossii* [Ideology and Politics in Post-Communist Russia] (Moscow: Editorial URSS, 2000), 115–29.

53 Alexei Yu. Zudin, "Rezhim Putina: kontury novoi politicheskoi sistemy" [The Putin Regime: Contours of the New Political System], *Obschestvennye nauki i sovremennost'* [Social Science and Modernity], no. 2 (2003): 67–83.

54 The absence of doctrinal ideology distinguishes this official public sphere substantially from its Soviet analogue, although it also supposes some implicit rules that restrict expression. It is noticeable that the restrictions are not as much clearly articulated as voluntarily accepted by the principal actors.

CHAPTER 5
THE TRANSFORMATION DECADE: MORE STATE THAN SOCIETY?

GEVORG POGHOSYAN

The social transformations following the breakup of the Soviet Union are remembered as the beginning of a new era. Events of this type often require time for social scientists and average people to apprehend and understand them. Social change and other consequences are already evident for a number of reforms that continue to be implemented. In this chapter, I contribute to the analysis of the reform outcomes, which politicians have labeled "transitional."

Western theories of modernization have recently undergone revision. The main idea behind this revision has been to account for the absence of a useful modernization model that can be applied to all countries on the way to "postindustrial" development. There are multiple paths to postindustrial society,[1] which follows the development of industrial capitalism.[2] Post-socialist countries involved in the process of social modernization experience serious difficulties, such as a partial decline in industrialization and even regression in certain sectors of the economy.

The "modernization rebound" and some deindustrialization comprise a common stage of post-socialist development. As a rule, the application of classical Western models of modernization to post-Soviet societies results in some social destruction. The problem lies in the absence of coherent models for direct inclusion of distinct ethnocultural variations and processes.

Many researchers believe that Soviet society embraced modernization, but that it could not continue and complete the process because of its closed, undemocratic nature, that is, government suppression of civil society, and hence the absence of a place for civil initiative and self-organization. The results of social reforms in post-Soviet countries are not yet clear, even to reformers and analysts. Whatever the final results will be, they will not precisely duplicate the course of Western development, because of the post-Soviet countries' unique political and economic history.

As American sociologist Neil Smelser notes, "The Russian evolution of the last decade will make us revise our overestimation of current theories of development."[3] American political economist Francis Fukuyama observes that "one of the basic problems in Poland, Hungary, Russia, Ukraine, and other former communist counties is in their trying to create democratic political institutions without having the privileges of a functioning capitalistic economy. The absence of enterprise, markets, and competition brings not only the aggravation of poverty, but impedes the forming of extremely necessary forms of public support for a proper functioning of democratic institutions."[4]

Almost all former communist countries suffer from a weakness of civil society that results, in part, from the centralization of authority in state institutions. Today, the post-Soviet states span a wide range of liberal, pseudo-liberal, and authoritarian regimes, suggesting that the development of institutions of civil society will continue to vary across the one-time Soviet space.

In every country of the former Soviet Union, the architects of post-Soviet modernization had neither a detailed general plan nor an articulated national concept of social reform. The process of transforming the economy thus became a stumbling block. Many countries experienced a" "modernization rebound" represented by a sudden decline in production, a loss of markets, a halt in enterprise-related activity, and an increase in mass unemployment, especially in the earliest period of reform. In the case of Armenia, for example, the" "modernization rebound" brought real deindustrialization to the country, moving it toward more archaic forms of economic activity, especially in agriculture.

The process of capital accumulation by private landowners was very slow. In addition, there was foreign private investment. After land reform, new landowners had to resort to manual labor while at the same time trying to achieve the same productivity as mechanized operations. Considerable subsistence agriculture was practiced by the population in both urban and rural locations. Sociological researchers provide evidence of land privatization that was executed in a manner that infringed on the economic rights of peasants.[5] The high rate of outmigration resulted in the "aging" of the rural population. As a result, one-third of private, arable land was left unused by small farmers or anyone else because of labor shortages.

Economic reforms in post-Soviet countries during the transition period can be divided into three stages: (1) the beginning of institutional reforms, (2) comparative stabilization and some macroeconomic growth, and (3) strategic change "from stabilization to development."

Concerning the strategy of industrial privatization, of the millions of certificates distributed gratis among the citizenry, practically all saw a decrease from their initial market value within several years. Most preferred to sell their certificates and not participate in the privatization process. As a result, certificates were concentrated in the hands of a small segment of the population (5 to 7 percent). During the Soviet era, the state sector had a near monopoly on ownership; in contrast, in the post-Soviet period, privatization resulted in property held by a small proportion of private owners. The unequal distribution of property has contributed to extreme poverty, and is an example of poor organization of the privatization process as well as bureaucratic unwillingness to allow ordinary citizens, the main participants in economic reform, to become involved in the privatization process. Property ownership concentration increased immensely, and the economic modernization process was effectively crippled. In Armenia, a sizeable middle class of private property owners has not emerged.

In the last decade of the 20th century, the strategy of post-Soviet modernization brought the former Soviet republics to deindustrialization and economic development rollback, resulting in a type of hybrid economy. The market economy became noncompetitive and monopolistic in many areas. I have found that the current model of economic transformation represents a post-socialist market without substantive free competition, which is managed largely by clans and state regulators. Western experts note that most post-Soviet countries are regarded as states with a middle level of economic development and "parasitical authoritarian governments."[6]

Social stratification reflects the results of implemented reforms, as well as likely future directions. Social structure is determined by a number of relatively static subsystems. Once social structural change occurs, it is long-lasting. As Russian scholar Tatiana Zaslavskaya has pointedly noted, social structure is the "solar plexus" of society.[7]

My research shows that ongoing structural changes in contemporary Armenian society are already striking. The following summarizes the social stratification results of the first phase of post-Soviet reform in Armenia[8]:

- *Upper*: political and economic elites, large business owners, and top managers of leading manufacturing and distribution corporations: 5 to 7 percent of the population

- *Upper-middle*: small private business owners and entrepreneurs, highly paid professionals, and state functionaries and managers: 10 to 12 percent

- *Majority*: office and other service sector workers, low-paid manufacturing and trades workers, schoolteachers and other education sector workers, small farmers and merchants, pensioners, and temporarily unemployed workers: 65 percent

- *Underclass/bottom*: homeless people, chronically unemployed people, sex service workers, and other social "outsiders": 15 percent

On the whole, Armenian society has become more fragmented, and the gaps between the living standards of the various social strata have increased many times over. There are more workers in commerce and services, and there are social groups or categories that did not exist in the former social structure (large business owners, and private business managers and investors, at one extreme, and homeless people, sex service workers, and social "outsiders" at the other). The growth social marginalization has begun. The transitional social structure is characterized by amorphousness, extreme instability, and uncertainty.

THE COLLAPSE OF LIVING STANDARDS, OR THE "NEW POVERTY"

The unprecedented growth of unemployment brought economic hardship to large numbers of people. I refer to this phenomenon as the "new poverty," the result of reforms and the breakup of the former economic system. In fact, such poverty was not characteristic of society throughout the Soviet period.

The "New Poverty" of the post-Soviet countries has nothing in common with the broad-based poverty of Third World nations. But current strategies and approaches for studying and overcoming or reducing this new poverty are, as a rule, based on the experience of Third World countries in which large segments of the population are chronically poor. Generally speaking, the poverty in those countries is characterized by long-term inadequate nutrition, illiteracy, high child mortality rates, and poor public sanitation. But none of these conditions are relevant to the phenomenon of post-Soviet "New Poverty," which affects populations with a high level of education, a good to reasonable health-care system, and a decent standard of living. Rather, the "New Poverty" has affected people who were relatively well off in the past, such as skilled and semi-skilled workers, state office workers, the intelligentsia, pensioners, and domestic workers.

The differentiating feature of the "New Poverty" is expressed in its relatively urban character. In contrast to the situation in Third World countries, where the worst poverty is often found in rural areas, in Armenia, for example, impoverishment appears to be common among residents of small and middle-sized towns. Forty-eight percent of Armenians are poor, and 16 percent are considered the "poorest." The Gini coefficient is 0.53, which indicates a high degree of economic inequality. The richest 20 percent of the population has 32 times more income than the poorest 20 percent. In fact, the richest 10 percent receive 46.2 percent of the national income.[9] Such extreme income inequity and the presence of large numbers of impoverished people impede economic development and make rapid growth difficult. In short, the economic reforms resulted in high levels of poverty, which, ironically, became a brake on further reforms.

The Armenian "New Poverty" includes significant numbers of "working poor," that is, people whose income is too low to provide them a living wage. The phenomenon of poverty among the employed vividly testifies to the fact that poverty cannot be defeated only with business growth and the simple reduction of unemployment. Moreover, assuming that the current social stratification system is long-lasting, future increases in gross domestic product (GDP) will not lead to an automatic reduction of poverty. Instead, future GDP growth will widen existing income disparities. Rich people become richer, and poor people become poorer.

The aging of Armenia is occurring because of high rates of outmigration and growth in the proportion of unemployed people. The exodus of younger and more economically active people has significantly changed the social and demographic structure of the population.

MIGRATION AND DEPOPULATION

For Armenia as well as the entire South Caucasus, the main historical trend of the last decade of the 20th century was depopulation. Unprecedented in scale, the historical process of depopulation in the countries of the South Caucasus was one of many negative results of the collapse of the communist empire. An estimated 3 million people left the three countries of the region (Armenia, Azerbaijan, and Georgia). The main reasons for outmigration were the economic crisis, extreme reduction in workplace and living standards, and armed conflicts in the region such as the war between Armenia and Azerbaijan over Karabakh, one repercussion of which has been the blockade of Armenian railways by Azerbaijan.

Taken together, the three countries have become a net exporter of both skilled and unskilled labor. The largest segment of migrants, which consists of people (mostly men) from 18 to 55 years of age with postsecondary technical or professional education. According to official statistics, 30 percent of the migrants are scientists, teachers, engineers, or other types of specialists.[10] One result of losing large numbers of educated workers has been an increase in the proportion of unemployed people and dependents such as recipients of public assistance (e.g., pensioners, children, and single mothers).

While initially the main cause of depopulation was outmigration, after several years a decline in the birth rate also became a factor. The marriage rate and average family size declined. Ethnic homogenization of the South Caucasus was one effect of the depopulation process. Members of minority nationalities who had lived in the three countries for many decades left the region along with native peoples. In addition to Armenians, Azerbaijanis, and Georgians, outmigration streams included Russians, Jews, Greeks, Ukrainians, and Germans. In Armenia, 97 percent of the population by 2010 was ethnic Armenian.[11] The growth of nationalist spirit in society, the ethnic homogenization of the elites, and the promotion of nationalist ideology alongside state policy are possible reasons for this trend, together with cultural consolidation. The growth of national self-awareness is typical in many societies in post-Soviet countries, which are now experiencing various kinds of national rebirth.

DEVELOPMENT OF A MULTIPARTY SYSTEM

After long years of domination by a single-party communist system, political parties, unions, coalitions, movements, and other groups with the potential for political agency have begun in many post-Soviet countries. In a break with the classical model of multiparty systems,[12] which assumes the presence of two, three, or sometimes four parties, a super-multiparty system has formed in post-Soviet societies featuring the presence of several dozen or even hundreds of parties. For example, in 2002 there were 114 registered political parties and unions in Armenia, 198 in Russia, 126 in Ukraine, 145 in Georgia, 40 in Kyrgyzstan, and 28 in Estonia.[13]

Party pluralism in post-socialist countries is the result of a special cultural, historical, and political situation in which legally unlimited political pluralism has taken the place of long-lived regimes under a single-party system. The majority of officially registered parties do not have a discernible role in the political life of the country, and many exist only on paper. Many parties consist of a small number of members and a single leader.

Parties are active only during elections; they almost disappear from the political sphere after parliamentary or presidential balloting. Sociological research I undertook over a 12-year period allowed for observation of the development of the Armenian electorate's attitudes toward well-known political parties.[14] On the whole, only a small proportion of the citizenry pay attention to these parties and their activities. In general, the attitude of citizens is negative: most feel no sympathy for any party.

In Armenia, the 2003 parliamentary elections demonstrated the strengthening of a new phenomenon. New labor groups such as administrative-political unions, including in their membership rolls numerous representatives of state administration and the ruling elite, appeared together with traditional political parties. Also, financial-economic interest groups began to take an active part in elections.

A developmental analysis of political parties leads to the conclusion that consolidation of active parties is likely around a few basic ideologies over the short term. I distinguish three basic ideologies: liberal-democratic, social-democratic (or renewed communist), and national-socialistic.

ESTABLISHMENT OF DEMOCRATIC ELECTIONS

There are major differences between the understanding of democracy in post-Soviet societies and in the West. First, democracy for the Westerner means the participation of citizens in decision-making processes on several levels of state management. Research under the aegis of the international project "Democracy and Local Governance"[15] shows that for citizens of former Soviet republics, democracy is above all the guarantee of various forms of freedom of action, such as freedom of speech, liberty of conscience, and freedom of movement.

Of all democratic rights, people in post-Soviet societies place the greatest value on freedom of speech and a free press. This is due to the incontestable achievement of democratic reforms after long years of Soviet political censorship. For instance, television broadcasts from around the world became available by satellite and cable.

Europeans think in categories of *participatory democracy*, while citizens of post-Soviet countries are satisfied with *representative democracy,* with their involvement in the political process consisting mainly of voting in elections. Between elections, citizens' participation in political processes is minimal. There are no nontraditional forms of political participation at all.[16] In fact, the authorities are not interested in attracting citizens to the real management of social and political life as advocated by liberal-democratic reformers.

My sociological surveys are evidence that ordinary citizens are not convinced that participation would enable them to affect the decision-making process. There is a high level of distrust toward democratic electoral institutions and strong skepticism about the possibility of the electorate having an influence on the outcome of elections. Such an attitude can be manifested in behavior I would characterize as that of the "protested electorate." In the 1991–2003 period, the electoral participation of citizens gradually declined. Today, social nihilism and a "crisis of confidence" characterize the content of relations between state and society in post-Soviet countries.

MEDIA FREEDOMS AND THE "FOURTH POWER"

According to my surveys, the main source of information for the overwhelming majority of citizens is television. After the Soviet period, the print media readership was drastically reduced. There are two main reasons for such a reduction: (1) the prohibitive cost of newspapers and magazines for most citizens; and (2) distrust of the newspapers themselves.[17] The problem of trust in mass media in the case of freedom of speech and freedom of the press is a key part of social consciousness in a society undergoing transformation.

Most mass media organs are privately owned. The result is that print media independence from government authorities has turned into dependence on political party founders or financial sponsors. Freedom of the press in such conditions is difficult to assess.

The formation process of the "fourth power" has been delayed. Two reasons for this are the small circulation of newspapers and lack of topics of interest to the (potential) readership, on the one hand. On the other, public opinion is not strong enough to exert sufficient pressure on the authorities. That is why the problems raised by the mass media often receive inadequate attention from the authorities.

THE EVOLUTION OF VALUES

The social sphere in general, and public opinion in particular, suffers from a distinct inertia, which is especially evident during periods of major change. The scale and tempo of economic and political reforms sometimes leave social transformation far behind.

In the former Soviet space, the direction and success of modernization will depend on how quickly society becomes ready to accept new values and models of organizing everyday life. The formation of new values is a very difficult and often internally contradictory process. It is a fundamental replacement of value systems and basic assumptions, which can occur on "the ruins of a fragmenting normatively valued system."[18]

In any case, the social consciousness of a certain part of Soviet society was ready to appreciate the values of democracy. European democracy looked attractive at first. However, disappointment soon set in. Survey results in the second half of the 1990s showed that disillusion with democratic values deepened with the growth of an "anarchic" tendency in society and with misfortunes resulting from economic reforms. Disappointment generated an atmosphere of nostalgia for the communist past. Moral relativism and the wish for an authoritarian "strong hand" characterize in part the moral-psychological state of the social consciousness of post-Soviet society.

Traditional values such as honesty, devotion, decency, and fairness became devalued. Pragmatism and social egotism usurped the pseudo-collective spirit. Strategies of personal success have begun to play a dominant role in mass behavior. Today, the values of family and individual environment are dominant in the consciousness of most people. Meanwhile, individualism has become deeper in terms of market relations.

THE TRANSFORMATIONAL RESOURCES OF SOCIETY

The experience of post-Soviet societies shows that a market economy can be combined with authoritarian political management. The point is that all reforms lie on the culture "matrix" of a society and incorporate public practice and local tradition. Implementation of the same transformational models varies from one sociocultural sphere to another.

Clearly, most people in post-Soviet societies did not comprehend and did not support the reforms of the transformation period. That is why the transition model of post-Soviet modernization did not get broad-based social support and could not attract the necessary social resources.

Social science research and analysis did not support the transitional reforms. Strange as it may seem, even though the post-Soviet countries possessed a solid potential, they failed almost entirely to provide a foundation for the reforms.

The faith in Western recipes and distrust of a given society's own scientific personnel provided the conditions for the final dismissal of scientists and technical experts from the processes of social transformation. This development underscores the *necessity for a national face to modernization theory, rather than something universal to all modernizing societies*. The development of democracy on the basis of a nation's historical and ethno-cultural peculiarities now seems to be a necessary condition.

Finally, socially specific cultural-historical and national features, on the one hand, and, on the other, global international conditions, will determine what type of modernization will be best suited to post-Soviet society. Still, post-Soviet countries today are more state than society.

The network structure of the coming social order is one of the essential characteristics of globalization.[19] The national model of modernization must be built with a sensitivity to the individual needs of each post-Soviet state. In the case of Armenia, for a long time the fate of Armenian diasporas has lain in a certain network structure that extends far beyond the borders of the Armenian state. The globalization century can become a period of productive integration into the new world order by means of realizing the network potential of these Armenian diasporas.

NOTES

1 Samuel Huntington, *The Clash of Civilizations and the Remaking of World Order* (New York: Simon & Schuster, 1996).

2 Daniel Bell, *The Coming of Post-Industrial Society: A Venture in Social Forecasting* (New York: Basic Books, 1973).

3 Neil J. Smelser, Sociology (Englewood Cliffs, NJ: Prentice Hall, 1994), 11–12.

4 Francis Fukuyama, *Trust: The Social Virtues and the Creation of Prosperity* (New York: Free Press, 1995), 155.

5 Gevorg Poghosyan, *Hay hasarakutyune XXI daraskzbin* [Armenian Society at the Beginning of the 21st Century] (Yerevan, Armenia: Lusabatz, 2006) (Armenian).

6 *Nations in Transition*, 2004 (Washington, DC: Freedom House, 2004).

7 Tatiana Zaslavskaya, "Sociostrukturnie aspekti transformacii rossiskogo obchestva" [Social Structural Aspects of Transformation in Russian Society], *Sociologicheskie issledovania* [Sociological Research] no. 8 (2001): 3–11.

8 Gevorg Poghosyan, *Sovremennoe Armyanskoe obchestvo. Osobennosti transformacii* [Contemporary Armenian Society: Peculiarities of Transformation] (Moscow: Academia, 2005).

9 Ibid. See also Gevorg Poghosyan, *Armyanskoe obchestvo v transformacii* [Armenian Society in Transformation] (Yerevan, Armenia: Lusabats, 2003).

10 Armen Papoyan and Nina Baghdasaryan, *O nekotorikh voprosakh migracii armyanskogo naselenia v Rossiu* [On Several Issues Regarding Armenian Population Migration to Russia] (Yerevan, Armenia: Statistica, 1999), 10.

11 See National Statistical Service of the Republic of Armenia, available at http://www.armstat.am.

12 Moris Dyuverzhe, *Politicheskie partii* [Political Parties] (Moscow: Academic Project, 2000).

13 *Nations in Transition 2002* (Washington, DC: Freedom House, 2002).

14 Gevorg Poghosyan and Samson Mkhitaryan, "Party Pluralism in Political Practice of Armenia," *Mkhitar Gosh* (Yerevan, Armenia) no. 4 (2004): 28–38.

15 Betty M. Jacob, Krzystztof Ostrowski, and Henry Teune, eds., *Democracy and Local Governance: Ten Empirical Studies* (Honolulu: Matsunaga Institute for Peace, University of Hawaii, 1993).

16 Alan Marsh, *Protest and Political Consciousness* (Beverly Hills, CA: Sage, 1977).

17 Gevorg Poghosyan, ed., *The Reading of Newspapers in Armenia* (Yerevan, Armenia: IREX/PROMEDIA/ASA, 2002).

18 *Dinamika cennostei naselenia v reformiruemoi Rosii* [The Dynamic of the People's Opinions for Reforming Russia] (Moscow: Editorial URSS, 1996), 44–45.

19 Gevorg Poghosyan, "*Globalnie tendencii mirovogo razvitia i perspektivi Kavkaza*" [Global Tendencies of World Development and Caucasus Perspectives]] *Obchestvo i Ekonomika* [Society and Economy] no. 10---11 (1999): 226–230.

CONCLUSION

BETH A. MITCHNECK

The chapters in the present volume constitute an effort to frame a conversation around state and society in the former Soviet space through a focus on cultural and political processes. Each author has taken a broad view to contribute theoretical observations to the greater conversation. As a whole, our authors understand social transformations in ways that are independent of the terms *transition* and *democratization*. Their observations about the particular context of the former Soviet Union are not contingent upon a transition to capitalism or democracy, but rather, upon historical processes of state and social engagement. This focus is distinct from a focus on civil society. Civil society is of course a critical part of the state–society relationship, yet the term itself diverts attention from the interrelationship between state and society to a particular form of social interaction. Inasmuch as we are interested in the interrelationship or interplay between notions of the state and society, our authors comment on social transformation from the broad perspective of connections, networks, and power within and around state and society.

STATE–SOCIETY RELATIONSHIPS DURING TIMES OF SOCIAL CHANGE

Painter's conceptualization of how the state acts and is a participant in the larger process of governance provides a foundation for the ways that both Malinova and Kradin understand state–society relations during times of change. By focusing on the state as a participant in social and power relationships rather than as the holder of all power, both Malinova and Kradin are able to engage state–society relationships as purveyors of change in a mutually constituted manner rather than regard one side of such relationships as subordinate to the other. While not denying state power, their use of the engagement between state and society helps advance a view of that relationship as more subject to multidimensional social interaction than is often found in the literature on the former Soviet Union.

Hanson refines the notion of state–society interaction by focusing on intellectual and state elites and their interactions around nationalism. He positions in the foreground the issue of multidimensionality of state–society relations and the role played by ideology. From this perspective, government is structured by those interactions, specifically interactions around the negotiation of ideologies. When ideology is less clear across intellectual and state elites, then the role of nationalism also becomes less coherent. Hanson does not directly address the role of "civil society" in the analysis of state–society relations, yet civil society becomes less salient as a negotiation site when the focus shifts to ideologies and communication across groups.

Painter's concept of "stateness," the performance of government, also moves us beyond civil society as an agent of change to the possibility of seeing individual action as the performance of change. Government can be performed outside of formal channels just as change can occur through stateness. From a theoretical perspective, the chapters by Hanson, Kradin, Malinova, and Painter help us focus on the imperative of considering state–society interactions as multidimensional and not unidirectional in terms of power to affect change.

CONCEPTUALIZING GOVERNANCE

Painter's proposal to use stateness to link individuals and action to the realization of the state through the performance of actions leads to the proposition, well-considered in the state theory literature but less so in the literature on the post-Soviet space, that the state exists only because of the interaction between society and individuals. While Kradin contributes enormously to the literature on Russia by tracing the importance of kin and clan relationships to the composition of state actors, his work also allows us to consider the role of kin-based networks in the ability of government to act or governance to occur. Kradin's work, then, is an empirical example of Rhodes' view that governance stems from interorganizational networks and the resulting allocation of resources and social control.[1] Kinship and clan relationships as seen through placement within government networks are important mechanisms by which resource allocation occurs. As Stoker says, the allocation of resources through networks blurs distinctions between state and civil society.[2] In the case of Russia, that blurring has resulted in the viewpoint that civil society in Russia is both only beginning and weak. Yet looking more broadly at the various ways in which state and society interact—beyond civil society—allows for new theorization of the multidimensionality of the state–society relationship.

The historical analyses of Kradin and Malinova suggest that interactions between state and society have occurred in very meaningful ways and have shaped governance. Both authors show how different forms of networking or communicating shape the networks within which governance occurs. Poghosyan shows the clear distinction of outcomes in Armenia relative to other cultural contexts. These are important building blocks for future theoretical work on state action in Russia and other former Soviet republics.

CONCEPTUALIZING CHANGE THROUGH NETWORKS

Following from Klijn and Skelcher's position that a focus on governance networks may help contextualize country-specific analyses,[3] all of our authors focus on the relativity of social change and interactions and contingency on specific cultural and historical processes—including communication and organization of and around networks. If we agree that governance occurs through networks, does it follow that networked governance is at play in the former Soviet Union and now in Russia and other countries? Parker's reminder that networked governance (e.g., coordination) is not governance through networks[4] brings attention back to the social relations embedded within networks and then the ways that individuals within networks interact to shape governance and resource allocation.

Governance networks describe a way for state and society to interact. Kradin's historical analysis of the ways that state and society are mutually constitutive over time provides a clear example of heterarchic networks described by Jessop[5] and the self-organization into state-like settings discussed by Painter. The social relationships that individuals bring to the self-organization of the state provide the power base on which individuals within the networks act. In Kradin's case, that power base comes from centuries of social relationships and the importance of the clan and kinship relationships to forming the power to act and self-organize. Kradin's detailed analysis of the embeddedness of clan and kin in the *nomenklatura* system is a form of social network analysis. Kradin's revelation that self-organization creates stateness through social networks describes a historical process that predates both communism and nationalism (see Hanson). Yet Hanson's embedding of nationalism within elites in positions of power opens a space for the theorization of nationalism being one potential outcome of governance networks within a certain set of conditions related to social transformation—rather than related to democratization.

Hanson and Malinova both focus on how and why ideas spread through segments of society—again, this spread of ideas is virtually independent of democratization and more dependent on the ways that state and society interact. Malinova's historical approach is a major contribution to the literature because she traces how meaning is attached to the dissemination of ideas—a topic that is neglected in the transitology literature. Her work shows how variable forms of networks, including communication through the Internet and other forms of mass media, are formative of how governance networks work.

Malinova's observation of multiple and overlapping social groups interacting in variable public spaces also fits well into theorization of the spread of political communication through networks. Framing political communication as occurring in a variety of ways and spaces underscores Poghosyan's key point that because of historical forms of social interaction around political processes, the spread of and engagement with political ideas does not necessarily need to take place within formal mechanisms of representative democracy, as this is not the political tradition in post-Soviet countries.

Our authors identify traditions of political discourse that stem from social practices that evolved long before communism. Kradin's disentangling of governance networks and networks of power highlights the importance of social and historical context to the process of governance. His theoretical contribution to understanding state and society lies in the framing of the power to act within governance networks as coming from the power associated with sociohistorical relationships—inextricably linking state and society in a way that creates multiple pathways for flows of power. This interaction between state and society leads to complex flows of power and social relationships that are both culturally and historically specific yet can be traced through various forms of networks.

NOTES

1   R.A.W. Rhodes, "The New Governance: Governing without Government," *Political Studies* 44 (1996): 652–67.

2   Gerry Stoker, "Governance as Theory: Five Propositions," *International Social Science Journal* 50 (1998): 17–28.

3   Erik-Hans Klijn and Chris Skelcher, "Democracy and Governance Networks: Compatible or Not?" *Public Administration* 85 (2007): 587–608.

4   Rachel Parker, "Networked Governance or Just Networks? Local Governance of the Knowledge Economy in Limerick (Ireland) and Karlskrona (Sweden)," *Political Studies* 55 (2007): 113–32.

5   Robert Jessop, "The Rise of Governance and the Risks of Failure: The Case of Economic Development," *International Social Science Journal* 50 (1998): 29–45.

ACKNOWLEDGEMENTS

The editor gratefully acknowledges the Carnegie Corporation of New York for their support of the Centers for Advanced Study and Education (CASE) Program and international workshops organized through the Kennan Institute. The opportunity for us to meet and collaborate in this project generated not only new collegial relationships for this immediate project, but also a series of ongoing intellectual dialogues and even friendships. We would like to extend our immense gratitude to Blair Ruble for his unflagging support of this project at all of its stages. The editor also greatly appreciates the assistance of staff at the Kennan Institute offices in both Washington, D.C., and Moscow, for their help in ushering this project through the workshops and publication process. The editor and the Kennan also thanks Mikhail Ilyin for his tremendous contributions throughout the workshop phase. Finally, a warm thank you is extended to all of our authors and workshop participants, who persevered beyond our intense and inspiring workshops through several rounds of dialogues, debates, and revisions.

THE CASE PROGRAM

The Kennan Institute, in partnership with the Carnegie Corporation of New York, the John D. and Catherine T. MacArthur Foundation, the Russian Ministry of Education, and the Moscow Public Science Foundation, established the Centers for Advanced Study and Education (CASE) program in 2000. The CASE program established nine thematic research centers at regional Russian universities in order to foster scholarship in the social sciences and humanities. It seeks to integrate Russian scholars into the international academic community through a system of individual research fellowships, library and publications support, and professional community-building efforts. The Centers have been administered jointly with the ISE Center (Information. Scholarship. Education.) since 2002. The program will end in 2012.

ABOUT THE CONTRIBUTORS

Nikolay N. Kradin is head of the political anthropology department of the Institute of History, Archaeology and Ethnology of the Russian Academy of Sciences, and Professor at Far-Eastern Federal University in Vladivostok. He headed field archaeological and ethnological expeditions in Russian Far East, Siberia, Mogolia, Central Asia, and China. Kradin is author of over 300 publications, including 9 monographs and over 30 edited and co-edited volumes in political anthropology, archaeology and anthropology of inner Asian pastoral nomads, including "Alternative Pathways to Early State" (1995 in co-authorship), *Political Anthropology* (3nd ed., 2010, in Russian).

Beth Mitchneck received her Ph.D. from Columbia University in 1990 and is currently a professor of geography at the University of Arizona. She has served as associate dean for academic affairs in the College of Social and Behavioral Sciences as well as interim dean. Her duties as associate dean included recruitment and retention of faculty and all other personnel matters. Her primary research interests are in governance and migration, with a focus on Russia and the Caucasus. She is currently the lead principal investigator on a collaborative and interdisciplinary grant from the National Science Foundation to explore and analyze the experience of forced migrants in the Caucasus through an in-depth study of social networks and livelihood strategies. A human geographer, formerly at the Brookings Institution, she is past president of the Russian, Central Eurasian, and East European Specialty Group of the American Association of Geographers, served on the advisory board of the Kennan Institute at the Woodrow Wilson International Center for Scholars, and chaired the Eurasian Studies Fellowship Committee at the Social Science Research Council. Her recent publications include "Governance and Land Use Decision-Making in Russian Cities and Regions," in *Europe-Asia Studies* (2007), and "Geography Matters: Discerning the Importance of Local Context," in *Slavic Review* (2005).

Olga Malinova, Dr. of Philosophy, is the leading fellow of the Institute of Scientific Information for Social Sciences, Russian Academy of Sciences and Professor of Political Science Department of the Moscow Institute of International Relations. She is an author and editor of several books and articles about nationalism and national identity, political discourse and political ideologies, including *Liberal Nationalism (the Middle of the Nineteenth – the Beginning of the Twentieth Century)* (Moscow: RIK Rusanova, 2000), *Russia and "the West" in the Twentieth Century: Transformation of Discourse About Collective Identity* (Moscow: ROSSPEN, 2009), Ideas and Symbolic Space of Post-Soviet Russia: Dynamics, *Institutional Environment*, Actors, ed. by Olga Malinova (Moscow: ROSSPEN, 2011, forthcoming).

Joe Painter is professor and head of the department of geography at Durham University, Durham, UK. He holds a B.A. in Geography from Cambridge University and Ph.D. in Geography from The Open University. His academic expertise lies in the field of political geography and he is the co-author with Alex Jeffrey of *Political Geography: An Introduction to Space and Power* (Sage, 2009). He has published widely on urban and regional politics and government, theories of territory, and the geographies of citizenship and the state. He has a particular interest in the relationship between the state and everyday life.

Stephen E. Hanson is the vice provost for international affairs and director of the Wendy and Emery Reves Center for International Studies at the College of William and Mary. Hanson received his B.A. from Harvard University (1985) and his Ph.D. from the University of California, Berkeley (1991). He served from 2000-2008 as the director of the Ellison Center for Russian, East European, and Central Asian Studies at the Jackson School of International Studies, University of Washington. He is the author of two books: *Post-Imperial Democracies: Ideology and Party Formation in Third Republic France, Weimar Germany, and Post-Soviet Russia* (2010); and *Time and Revolution: Marxism and the Design of Soviet Institutions* (1997), in addition to being the co-author and co-editor of several other volumes. He has been a visiting scholar at the Minda de Gunzburg Center for European Studies at Harvard, a visiting scholar at the department of politics and international relations at Oxford University, and a research scholar at the

Kennan Institute at the Woodrow Wilson International Center for Scholars in Washington, D.C.

Gevorg Poghosyan is the president of the Armenian Sociological Association and director of the Institute of Philosophy, Sociology and Law at the Armenian National Academy of Sciences. He received his B.A. (1974), as well as his Doctor of Sociology (2003), from Yerevan State University. Poghosyan has served as a member of several organizations, including the International Academy of Sciences of Nature and Society; the International Philosophical Association; the International Sociological Association; the European Sociological Association; and as a member of the international board of editors of the Moscow-based magazine *Sociological Studies*. His main areas of research include issues of the methodology of sociology; verification of sociological information; elaboration of the theories of disaster, migration, and political sociology; as well as the peculiarities of societies during transitional periods.